THE LAST WORLD

Richard Spiegel

THE
LAST
WORLD

Astrolog Publishing House

Cover design: Na'ama Yaffe

© Astrolog Publishing House 2002
ISBN 965-494-126-0

Astrolog Publishing House
P. O. Box 1123, Hod Hasharon 45111, Israel
Tel: 972-9-7412044
Fax: 972-9-7442714
E-Mail: info@astrolog.co.il
Astrolog Web Site: www.astrolog.co.il

All rights reserved. No part of this publication may be reproduced, stored in a retrieval system, or transmitted in any form or by any means, electronic, mechanical, photocopying, recording or otherwise, without the prior permission of the publisher.

Published by Astrolog Publishing House 2002

Printed in Israel
1 3 5 7 9 10 8 6 4 2

TO DARLING DIANA

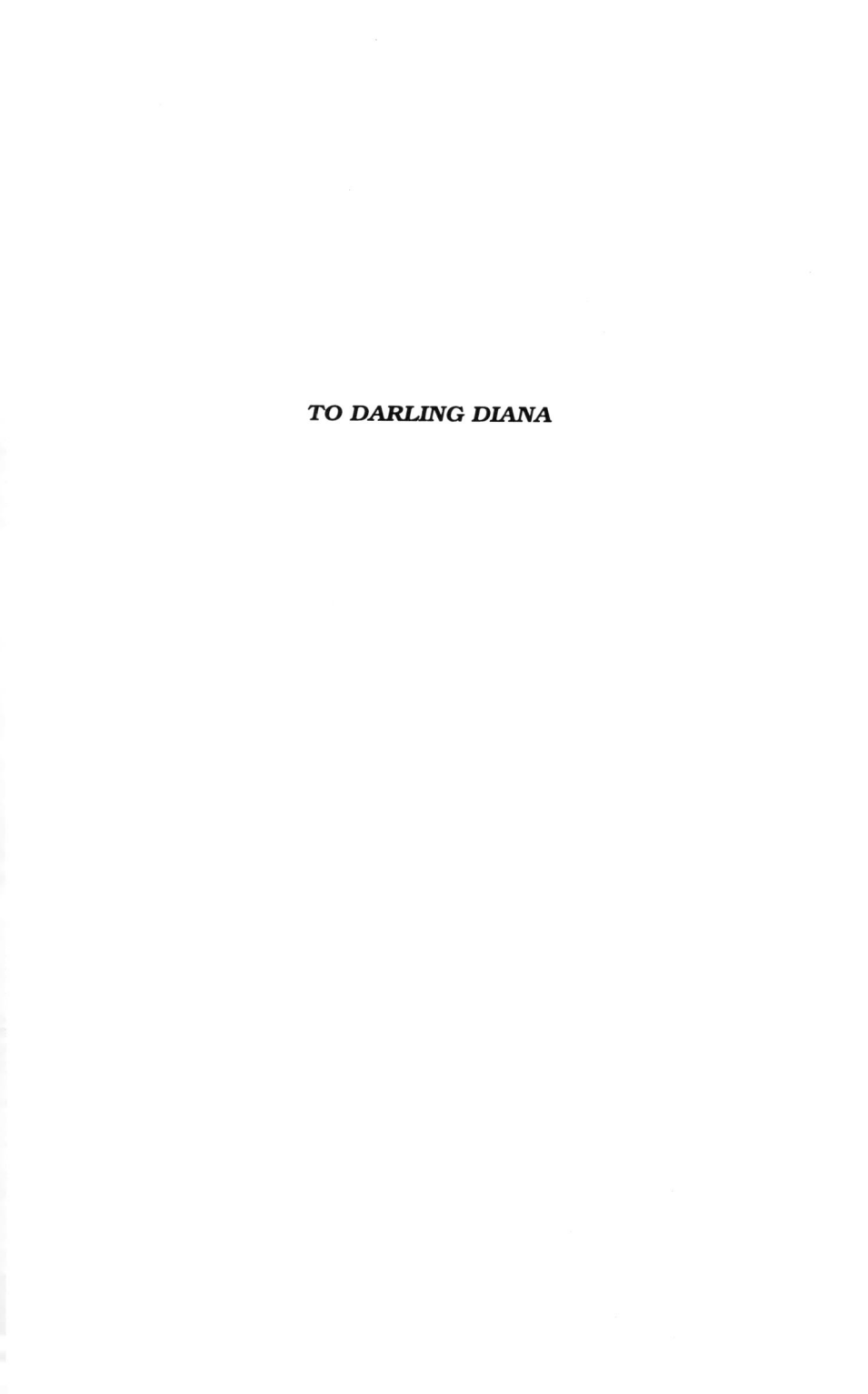

CONTENTS

Preface	9
Environ-Mentality	14
Seasons in the Heart	22
Not in My Back Yard	31
"The World is a Sacred Vessel"	39
Aristotle's Child	49
Carry the Yin, Embrace the Yang	55
On the Way	66
The Golden Extremes	70
Touch the Country	80
"Be the Pattern of the World"	91
The Useless Tree	97
A Mental Fear of Space	106
The Third Side of Life	118
The Spirit of Logic	129
The River Calls	140
"Among the Clouds of the Tempest"	149
Everyday Ways	159
Making My Teh	166
Intuitively	175
The Resurrection of Space and Time	194

Preface

In the summer of 1992, I took a break between jobs and sat down on my back deck to look over my lawn. It turned out to be a long look, taking nearly a decade. I looked at the front lawn as well. Sitting there that first summer, it occurred to me that I needed to show myself that I could tackle the smallest problem in my own yard before assuming I could solve or resolve the much larger issues that were - and always have been - occupying my mind. You know... the usual questions of life and the meaning thereof. So I started writing. The smallest issues were right before my eyes, but they turned out to be the deepest of all.

What has resulted, I hope, from the story of my efforts to balance both the lawn and my own life, is a practical, informal and easy-to-read description of the spirit of the Chinese philosophy of Taoism, and its Native American "cousins" and other scattered relatives.

The thread running through the text is a problem that seems so "suburban" as to be banal: the battle I have been having with my lawn - anthills all over the front yard, erosion taking over the back. How I learn to deal with these equal and opposite problems leads me to many relevant philosophies and religious principles from East and West and in between. How not to do battle and yet "win" is the most difficult and also the most necessary concept/behavior we can realize in an age of increasing social, economic, and ecological violence.

But written words themselves cannot be the Way. So I try to present a fresh approach to Taoism through storytelling: you will read and hear stories taken from both Eastern and Western traditions or Ways of life, the latter including Hermetic philosophy and the more traditional philosophies of Plato, Nietzsche, and Thomas Merton. Add to these some tales from indigenous Americans, with viewpoints unique to the New World. All of these tales are brought down to earth, literally, in my own storyline about the lawn and me.

When I began this book, I did not realize the possible connections between Taoism and Native American thought (that of the indigenous peoples of the Americas). And I do not want to overstress that conceptual connection, for there are profound differences as well, as there are even between Native philosophies themselves to this day. Yet, both Taoism and indigenous American Ways of life had insights that the European culture did not have as it was becoming dominant.

In fact, the European-based attitude toward the overcontrol of nature and other people - as opposed to reasonable control just over our selves - has evolved only slowly over the centuries, and all life on Earth will pay for that in this new millennium, no doubt. But the book before you is not "millennial" or alarming. It is more like a gateway to the year 2000 that traces a converging path back to ancient Ways. This path I call Wayfaring, and it grows out of both Taoism and several of its Western kin, taken metaphorically.

Whether this path backward (in order to move forward) is historically, not just logically convergent is for others to address. It is true that Native American populations are thought to stem from parts of Asia many thousands of years ago, drifting from Siberia across to Alaska and eventually down through the receding glaciers into the Americas. Or across the Pacific by boat.

In any case, it is intriguing to wonder if some of the connections I make between ancient Chinese and indigenous American approaches might just be peeling off the layers of time... and of space. This possible convergence of ancient East and West is being taken seriously by students of the Maya civilization and other great cultures of Mesoamerica.

By grappling with my need to make daily decisions - not just about my lawn but also about my relationships with people, animals and plants, my careers and my efforts to help slow down the erosion of nature itself - I try to show how practical Taoism and its Western and other relatives can be in helping to balance our own complicated existence. That needed harmony is not just between human beings, but also between ourselves and all other living things. But it is all but impossible to help balance the world out there if our own sense of time and space is out of sync.

Work is one big part of our daily existence that we know in our gut is distorted. More than 100 years ago, Nietzsche foresaw this situation as he foresaw so many of the other travails of the century that was to follow him. The "breathless haste" of Americans at work, he said, "... is spreading a lack of spirituality like a blanket. Even now one is ashamed of resting, and prolonged reflection almost gives people a bad conscience." Almost.

In the following reflections, I have relied on the classical writings and stories of many cultures.

It will be clear to readers that I have depended in particular on two translators of Taoist classics:

John C. H. Wu, for his translation of: *Tao Teh Ching* (Shambhala Dragon Editions, Shambhala Publications, Inc., Boston: 1989; copyright 1961 by St. John's University Press, New York) and cited in my text as the *Tao*.

Thomas Cleary, for the following works: *The Essential Tao*: An Initiation into the Heart of Taoism through the Authentic *Tao Te Ching* and the Inner Teachings of *Chuang Tzu* (Harper Collins, New York: 1991; copyright 1991 by the author), cited in part as the *Chuang Tzu*;

The Art of War of Sun Tzu (Shambhala Dragon Editions,

Shambhala Publications, Inc., Boston: 1988; copyright 1988 by the author), cited as the *Sun Tzu*;

Vitality, Energy, Spirit: A Taoist Source Book (Shambhala Dragon Editions, Shambhala Publications, Inc., Boston: 1991; copyright 1991 by the author), and cited as *VES*;

Further Teachings of Lao-tzu: Understanding the Mysteries (Shambhala Publications, Inc., Boston: 1991; copyright 1991 by the author), cited as the *Wen Tzu*;

The Tao of Politics: Lessons of the Masters of Huainan (Shambhala Dragon Editions, Shambhala Publications, Inc., Boston: 1990; copyright 1990 by the author), cited as Huainanzi;

Immortal Sisters: Secrets of Taoist Women (Shambhala Publications, Inc., Boston: 1989; copyright 1989 by the author), cited as *IS*.

Most of the chapter, "Among the Clouds of the Tempest," originally appeared as "The Pre-Columbian Mind: Among the Clouds of the Tempest" in *The Quest*, Winter 1992. The core of the chapter on "The Spirit of Logic" first appeared as an article in *Philosophic Research and Analysis*, Summer 1978 and was collected in the volume, *Philosophy of the Humanistic Society* (The Institute of Advanced Philosophic Research, 1981).

Of course, it is impossible to acknowledge the many Western influences on me. In the Western world, there is often warfare between spirit and matter, soul and nature, people and other living things. D. H. Lawrence embodied much of this typical warfaring, and yet when he visited Northern New Mexico in the early 1920s he had an insight into what I call Wayfaring: "...actually *touch* the country, and you will never be the same again."

And we must touch it very soon, before "we have buried so much of the delicate magic of life." (Alex Shoumatoff, *Legends of the American Desert*: Sojourns in the Greater Southwest: Knopf, 1997, pp. 18-19, cited below as *LAD*)

Lawrence asserted his view at a time when substantial portions of the cultures and physical environment associated with traditional peoples were less damaged than now. But decades later, at the opening of the new millennium, these cultures are still hanging on while the environment itself is seen more than ever as separated from us. This is a time when human domination is generating uncontrolled responses - social chaos, resource entropy, and globe-circling disease - more than equal to it in power. Wayfaring attempts to reduce our warfare with nature.

This is what the Hopis call the "last world" - our last chance to get it right.

But if Nietzsche is on target, the eternal recurrence of the cyclical universe of matter guarantees us at least this one additional chance, but there is a real danger that it might come too late.

All these insights show that the East has no monopoly on wisdom. The poorly known relatives of such Eastern paths as Taoism have been in our own backyard for centuries. Even the better-known influences on the West occasionally have kinship with Taoism, as Merton reminds us so eloquently. I was reminded again of that truth just the other day, when I read this passage from the Bible (Job 12:7-8):

Ask the beasts, and they will teach you;
the birds of the sky, they will tell you;
or speak to the earth, it will teach you;
the fish of the sea they will inform you.

However we frame the issues discussed in this book, where there is a will, there is a Way, but we ourselves have to find it. We can then move forward in time and space just as the lawn does.

Richard Spiegel

Richard Spiegel

Environ-Mentality

Ants at the Front

One week ago I came back from a California vacation to find thousands of small ocher anthills all over the front yard of our rolling three-quarters of an acre in Maryland. That got me thinking.

I went to the local nursery for advice. The owner was asleep at his desk in the back room when I came in, but a young female clerk woke him briefly to pass along my urgent plea for help. His reply: apply a pesticide containing Diazinon.

Same answer from the friendly people at the nearby hardware store. I read the label on the sack of pesticide: it duly warned that birds may die if they ingest the Diazinon.

You don't have to be a Taoist to regard that result as overkill. So I asked around for more natural ways to combat the militarily industrious ants. "Find an anteater," said one man at the hardware store. Clearly I had to do more than just think. I had to do something, right now.

Man follows the ways of the Earth.
The Earth follows the ways of Heaven,
Heaven follows the ways of Tao,
Tao follows its own ways.
                    (*Tao*, 25)

When I got back to the battlefield, I carried with me not sandbags but bags of seed of dark-green fescue grass. I spread the seeds all over, then watered them down. My thought was to use the fast-growing grass to overpower the ants: perhaps the seed, prepared with thousands of now-wet anthills, would take hold at each site, blend in with the existing grass, and push out the ant-invaders.

Yesterday my wife and I each watered the seedlings. This morning I went out to check things and what I saw astonished me: right next to every mudspot, the ants had - overnight - rebuilt each sandy home. It was an all-out, masterfully coordinated, and silent counterattack.

Today I am still at war with the tiny soldiers; I'm armed with only a hose with weak water pressure and one million seeds, each promising dark-green, hardy, and speedy growth. Because the number of seeds just about matches the ants one-for-one, what else do the ants have, and similarly what weapons do I have, that might give one side an advantage?

Not determination: that too is equal on both sides - the ants' one million little stubborn attitudes vs. my one very great determination, which I estimate to be one million times the force of a single ant's, but overall roughly equal to the sum of the forces of all the ant-attitudes.

It all comes down to this: the ants' organization and discipline are their advantage; the technology of water-through-the-hose is mine.

Nothing in the world is softer and weaker than water; But, for attacking the hard and strong, there is nothing like it! For nothing can take its place.

(*Tao*, 78)

Water searches for its own lowest level, at least water in its natural state does. As it searches, usually downhill, it sidesteps obstacles in its way, such as boulders or (again usually) whole villages. It does not confront obstacles but rather wears them down, and Heraclitus would say we can know that time exists just by watching the one-way flow of a river.

This is water-action in nature. Of course sometimes water can turn violent, but only when another element leads the way, as wind (air) does in a storm or soil (earth) does in a flood. Water also naturally offsets the element of fire.

But it is human technology that brought all these ants to my front door. Our hilly yard beckoned them after other potential home sites for them were paved over by humans in search of their own bedroom suburbs.

I understand all that but I still want my yard back. So here I have in my hand the apex of garden-hose technology, this pale-green 50-foot plastic hose through which passes the water of life, forced by physical laws to rush out the far end under pressure (well, some pressure), having a specified direction and momentum in phase space quantifiable by Cartesian coordinates as interpreted by Newtonian laws.

What can I do with this liquid voltage? Or should I just leave the ants alone, leave them in peace, and walk away from this uphill fight? These indeed seem to be my options in the real world: fight with violent arms (pesticides); cope by using natural means such as water (fire is not a legal option); or just forget the whole thing, turn away and let the ants have my yard.

Get Wisdom: Go to the ant thou slugg and Delay not.

(From the *Penmanship Drill Book* of 1898, in the Historic Shepherdstown Museum, Shepherdstown, West Virginia)

A Just War

The violence scenario initially appeals to me as apparent justice: the militaristic ants meet their Waterloo. My cause seems to fit the medieval criteria for a just war. In addition, I am a human being, after all, and these are only a million dumb little crawling (or marching) insects. They will surely take over after the future nuclear holocaust so often referred to in the *Star Trek* programs.

Fine weapons of war augur evil.
Even things seem to hate them.
Therefore, a man of Tao does not set his heart
    upon them.

(*Tao*, 31)

But using deadly pesticides means certain death for innocent birds, our closest allies in the struggle against insect encroachment. Birds play a key role in a healthy ecology, they sing most beautifully (especially in the very early morning) and, in any case, they were here first.

The accumulation of pesticides is extremely harmful, and specifically carcinogenic, to people. It is especially dangerous to use pesticides on my hill, from which the stuff can seep down to other homes, contaminate the main water table and eventually disrupt both the Chesapeake Bay and the Atlantic Ocean.

How do we link up the environment "out there" with the human (or divine) mind "in here"?

Is this not the time to stop?
To know when to stop is to preserve ourselves from
    danger.
The Tao is to the world what a great river or an ocean
is to the streams and brooks.

(*Tao*, 32)

Multiply my violent scenario by millions and it becomes apparent that it is wrong to attack the ants with such chemicals. And less potent chemicals won't work.

> *Heaven-and-Earth is not sentimental;*
> *It treats all things as straw-dogs.*
> *(Tao, 5)*

Am I being too soft-minded here? I don't think so, because just to leave these ant-heap-builders alone, to let the value-neutral straw-ants take over my property completely, is to assure misery for my wife and for me. New sod is too expensive, and a bare honey-colored yard of blowing sand will get us into moral, financial, and legal hassles with our neighbors, local government, and the police. I can imagine the anthill wasteland expanding to all our neighbors' lawns and beyond.

So I am left with the waterhose option or something like it.

> *The highest form of goodness is like water.*
> *Water knows how to benefit all things without striving*
>   *with them.*
> *It stays in places loathed by all men.*
> *Therefore, it comes near the Tao.*
> *(Tao, 8)*

Watercourse

Before I proceed with this watercourse (a version, perhaps, of the ancient Chinese water torture), it occurs to me that applying water might actually make things worse. What if the ants just drink it all in and somehow use it to make even more hills with which to surround our home?

To hasten the growth of life is ominous.
To control the breath by the will is to overstrain it.
To be overgrown is to decay.
All this is against Tao,
And whatever is against Tao soon ceases to be.
(Tao, 55)

Perhaps encouraging ant overdevelopment might eventually lead to ant reduction. If the ants construct too many sand hills, they will deprive themselves of the grass, weeds, and topsoil they need for survival.

Something like this has happened before. The lower crescent of the Mediterranean Sea, a desert today, was once lush with forests. The Romans, among many other imperial peoples, devastated and finally obliterated the forests with their need for firewood and tall timbers for ships. The spreading desertification was (and is) the result, contributing to the Roman Empire's famous fall. Easter Island may have been another example of environmental abuse leading to the collapse of human communities, at least according to Clive Ponting's *A Green History of the World: The Environment and the Collapse of Great Civilizations* (St. Martin's: 1992). Again:

For to be over-developed is to hasten decay,
And this is against Tao,
And what is against Tao will soon cease to be.
(Tao, 30)

Too bad they didn't have a "green" movement back then. I am a professional fundraiser, and I have to believe that the *Tao Teh Ching*'s advice to the Easter Island Wilderness Fund and to the Roman Conservancy would have been: "Pitch your direct-mail appeals to survival." Appealing to values (aesthetics, for example) works a little, and so does appealing to improving our happiness or income - but it is our own individual existence that we care most about and by extension the sustainability of our culture.

In any case, it looks now as if the water treatment is right for my ants. Either it will germinate the grass seeds and hopefully replace the ant-homes or it will encourage overdevelopment, hypergrowth and eventually the ants' self-destruction. Of course it is also possible that the watercourse will have no effect at all, but that is a risk I take in this water-driven approach.

Bend and you will be whole.
Curl and you will be straight.
Keep empty and you will be filled.
Grow old and you will be renewed.
            (*Tao*, 22)

But again, why take any action at all? Would it not be more Taoistic to do nothing? The answer appears to be No. Complete passivity and refusal to make choices is (as William James said) itself to make a choice for certain outcomes. I am choosing the wasteland option if I refuse to act against the ants. And that option would wreak pain on the humans in this neighborhood, not excluding my wife and myself...

I'm guessing, though, that there is a big difference between the micro-level of life the ants enjoy and the macro-level where humans and other large critters dwell. The ants seem to keep inventing and reinventing their communities. But people and trees, bears and deserts can't rebuild habitats overnight. Or even over a century, or from one millennium to the next.

The lost world of the ancient Taoists and the "last world" of the Hopi - this world, here and now, our last chance to get it right, to find a planetary balance - might be found right here in my own yard. I won't really know until I look beneath the surface of things.

Speaking of that, I have just now finished overseeding and watering the front lawn. It rained a bit, which should help - my side, I hope. Next, in accordance with my strategy, I put on my heaviest boots and walk all over the lawn, pressing the million seeds down into the welcoming mud hills beneath which a million ants cower in my wake.

Seasons in the Heart

Not Warfaring

What I will be calling "Wayfaring" - following the Way, the *Tao* - is going with nature: avoiding violence to our natural environment whenever and wherever we can. Taoism is not the only way to Wayfare, but its simplicity and straightforwardness are definite advantages over most other philosophical and religious guidelines for relating to nature.

In a word, Wayfaring is the opposite of warfaring against nature. This is true whether we are dealing with lawns or human lives.

Taoism is one major historical root of Zen Buddhism. Twenty-five hundred years is a long time, and numerous translations and interpretations of the *Tao* (pronounced like the first word in "Dow Jones") have come down to us and are still being published. But while Zen is usually grasped in terms of what Westerners would call a method or technique for achieving the non-goal of enlightenment, Taoism is construed as a teaching, a body of wisdom, a set of principles by which to guide one's life.

The chief sources of this universal teaching include: the *Tao Teh Ching* of Lao Tzu, which provides 81 chapter-poems on the arts of living and choosing; the *Chuang Tzu*, especially the first seven chapters known as the Inner Chapters, which extends the scope of the *Tao*; the *Wen Tzu* (also known as Understanding the Mysteries), which expounds on the meaning of the Tao; the *Art of War* of *Sun Tzu*, the Chinese classic on the art of competing with other states and, indirectly, other individuals; and the *Huainanzi*, or the Masters of Huainan, which offers advice on the art of making and keeping the peace.

When I say that Taoism is not the only way to go along

with nature, I am thinking of suppressed or underground traditions in Western history such as the non-European Wayfarers, now known as Native or indigenous Americans, American Indians, first peoples or first nations.

Christopher Columbus could not comprehend - and he apparently admitted so in his diaries - the non-aggressive attitude of the Taino people of the islands he called the Indies. "They are the best people in the world and above all the gentlest," Columbus wrote. "These islands are very green and fertile and the air very sweet." To him the point was that they were mere islands.

On the continent, meanwhile, the Plains Indians, who depended on the tepee, had designed it to fit in with the dominant elements, especially the wind, sun and cold. "The weather means the seasons," says *Sun Tzu*, and the tepee of the plains was truly seasonal. With its semi-circular cover pulled over a conical frame of straight poles,

...[t]he tepee was generally pitched with its back toward the prevailing westerly wind direction, its wide base and sloping sides giving high stability to the sometimes sudden and strong winds which occur on the plains.
(Colin F. Taylor, "The Plains," in *The Native Americans*; Smithmark: 1991, p. 67. Taylor is also Editorial Consultant.)

In choosing your dwelling, know how to keep to the ground.
(*Tao*, 8)

Of such Wayfarers, the *Wen Tzu* says:

The capabilities of vitality and spirit elevate them to the Way, causing vitality and spirit to expand to their fullest effectiveness without losing the source. Day and night, without a gap, they are like spring to living beings. This is harmonizing and producing the seasons in the heart.
(*VES*, p. 30)

But why hark back to a time that appears simpler and simplistic to us? We don't really want to go back to a life without medicine or surgery, hygiene or packaged food, airplanes, cars, or air conditioners, do we? Columbus lived before the revolution in Romantic sensibility, which in turn was a reaction, in part, to the previous, rationalistic Enlightenment (a hardworking word also used to translate the nonrationalistic essence of Zen).

Yet the *Tao* came much earlier than either the Romanticism of the early 19th century or Columbus' landfall on the Americas. The Taoist love of nature and nonviolent attitudes toward all natural things are not romantic conceptions at all but hard-nosed and bottom-line. They concern our survival, period. And the survival of something as unimportant as my front and back yards.

> *Does anyone want to take the world and do what he wants with it?*
> *I do not see how he can succeed.*
>
> (*Tao*, 29)

The Way of Way

The Taoist idea of nature is an ancient and still-viable option to the Western concept that Bill McKibben, in *The End of Nature* (Anchor: 1989, pp. 64-65), declares dead: nature as separate from and independent of human society.

In fact some historians claim that until recently nearly all European mind-sets have been hostile to dark woods, lofty mountains, scorched deserts, dense swamps and rushing rivers. In particular, some say that it is the Christian tradition that, harking back to the Garden of Eden, has feared nature, natural functions, wild animals, overgrown plants, tempting fruit, and slithering snakes.

Some critics, such as Kirkpatrick Sale, author of *The Conquest of Paradise: Christopher Columbus and the Columbian Legacy* (Knopf: 1990; from which I cited Columbus' "diaries" above), maintain that fear and loathing of the natural environment may also help explain the Western discomfort with the subject of sex.

Bill McKibben does find pro-nature passages in the Bible, especially in the story of Job, which counterbalances Genesis. But remember that before modern science and technology, life in Europe was a battle for balanced nutrition and protection from famine, flood, drought, and disease.

All of these attacks at least appeared to come from nature herself. In the eyes of pre-scientific Europeans, it was a case of the human male vs. female nature. For example, in European legend, Sir Gawain and other male knights had to cross treacherous marshes while searching for the Holy Grail (an emerald vessel, i.e. green). A marsh is the natural intersection of two elements that many cultural traditions, old and new, consider to be "female" - earth and water.

During the Middle Ages, the harshness of nature was summed up in the popular expression, "an unkindness of ravens," when those large black birds were seen as portents of the misery to come from death by the plague. In the old days, "unkind" meant "unnatural" (imagine that), as in dying from the plague. Gradually, it became a way of referring to groups of actual ravens.

In the Old World, it was nearly impossible to be kind to nature because nature was not *kin*, not experienced as intimately related to people; and nature herself did not appear to be kind to people. But, as Simon Schama shows in *Landscape and Memory* (Knopf, 1995), the demonizing of nature was not universal, nor is it even slightly persuasive any longer. And there *was* one European Way of kindness toward nature, and that was witchcraft.

For the last 100 years, the pagan movement called Wicca, though still underground, has resuscitated and tried to preserve pre-Christian traditions focusing on the magic implicit in nature. Because all witchcraft is polytheistic, it was and is a threat to established Western philosophies and religions, which are officially monotheistic, though in practice perhaps not entirely so. To put down witches' reverence for nature, the establishment has always attempted to brand them as "satanic," which is impossible, in that witches don't even believe in the final dualism of good vs. evil, much less in its personification (ultimately from the Middle East) as two gods or forces locked in perpetual opposition.

The New World of the Americas offered the Europeans one more chance at nature as Eden. At least there appeared to be unlimited building materials and fuel (from trees), new forms of very nutritious crops (corn, potatoes, sweet potatoes), new medicines (quinine, coca), new luxuries (tobacco, peppers, chocolate) and vast stretches of land to provide personal property and security. All of this growth was the true City of Gold; as the Europeans after 1492 searched for gold with ever more violent desperation, they stomped and marched over much greater wealth. They never found El Dorado because they were already there. We have found it too: right here.

One major reason for the harmony the Indians enjoyed with nature was their relatively smaller populations surrounded on all sides by vast resources. With the Europeans came not only increased numbers of people but also deadly diseases to the new world. Thrown out of balance, the immune systems of the indigenous peoples were shocked and overcome. Ever since, in the view of Robert Pirsig, the world of *values* has become more and more divided between what he calls the "European" and the "Indian" value systems (*Lila: An Inquiry into Morals*; Bantam: 1991; much more on this later) - with the values of and for nature caught between the two. We have already noted some of the Ways that display this kindness of values.

But when natural resources (is there any other kind?) are fought over, and where competition is forced on us by demand greatly overbalancing supply of basic goods, ethics (on the individual level) and politics (on the societal level) enter the picture. We live in such times; and we can never return completely to indigenous ways, even if we wanted to, because the supply from finite nature can never again keep up with the demand by the always-increasing population.

However, the Taoism of the East may be as relevant to Wayfaring as indigenous Ways are, for it was forged in times of terrible conflict and competition for the necessities of life. And Taoism upheld the Way of nature even under the most difficult circumstances in ancient China. In fact, those original Wayfarers claimed that such times are the result of the human propensity to throw nature off track, out of kilter; to play bully in the fields of the Lord... or in Hopi terms, "Koyaanisqatsi."

Wayfaring may be the best way out of the warfare between humans and nature. We might as well try it, for if we persist in seeing ourselves in primal conflict with nature, nature will ultimately win that war. Even if we humans win all the battles through technology, we will still lose everything. This "eco-logic" is inescapable, and is captured in a Taoist parable about some of their deities:

> *The lord of the south sea was Abrupt; the lord of the north sea was Sudden.*
> *From time to time Abrupt and Sudden got together in the territory of Primal Unity, and Primal Unity treated them very well.*
> *Abrupt and Sudden planned to repay Primal Unity's kindness.*
> *They said, "People all have seven openings, through which they see, hear, eat, and breathe; Primal Unity alone has none. Let us make openings in Primal Unity."*
> *So every day they gouged out a hole. After seven days, Primal Unity died.*
> (*Chuang Tzu*, Chapter 7, p. 120)

Notice that word "kindness" again. But let me make it clear right away: I am not thinking about a Romantic return to nature that represents an idyllic dream that never happened (or can happen) on Earth. The classic "social contract" philosophers thought of the natural state as a theoretical construct that helps to justify certain social and legal restrictions on people's behavior (different behaviors according to the different thinkers).

What Jacob Needleman (more on his views later on) has called "metaphysical ethics," the attempt to connect the nature of the universe with our ethical behavior - that's what I will meditate on, not a list of recommendations to give to you, or anyone else, on exactly what you should or should not be doing with your moral choices.

Here's another example of metaphysical ethics, a different approach to Chuang Tzu's Primal Unity. In a National Gallery of Art exhibition, "Olmec Art of Ancient Mexico," these ancient artists working over 3,000 years ago were shown expressing the possibility of new combinations of living creatures, part human and part animal, especially the jaguar.

Apparently an Olmec shaman was seen as capable of gradually transforming himself into a jaguar.

The Maya had a term for this, which in their language is read as *way*, a glyph which, according to Michael D. Coe in *The Maya* (Thames and Hudson, 6th ed.: 1999, p. 229),

> *still remains in use among many Maya groups for an individual's alter-ego spirit or co-essence, conceived as an animal counterpart (which might be anything from a jaguar to a mouse)..., each ruler had such a way, often a fantastic chimera combining the features of two or three animals, with whom he was in a special kind of relationship.*

But the most interesting part of this, from the perspective of metaphysics, is the ethical possibility it suggests: that Primal Unity is possible when we as humans remember our animal side. We have met the awesome jaguar of the tropical jungle, and like William Blake's Tiger in the night, he is us.

But so is a less-than-awesome animal partner, like a mouse, or an ant. Or even a fly, as in Blake's poem, "The Fly":

Little Fly,
Thy summer's play
My thoughtless hand
Has brush'd away.

Am not I
A fly like thee?
Or art not thou
A man like me?

For I dance,
And drink, and sing,

*Till some blind hand
Shall brush my wing.*

*If thought is life
And strength and breath;
And the want
Of thought is death;*

*Then am I
A happy fly,
If I live
Or if I die.*

Not In My Backyard

My Backyard

But all this gets very complicated when I try to apply it to my own yard. For just as every problem has at least two sides to it, my property has both a front yard and a backyard.

Although the front lawn is being overrun by mere ants - no jaguars in sight - the backyard is another problem. It is a hill that rises steeply with thick weeds surrounding all sides of a cliff-like eroded wall of clay-like soil that cuts straight across the middle of the yard.

The people who used to own this property tore down, for no apparent reason, a wall of heavy timbers supported by "deadmen," railroad ties jutting out perpendicularly from the bare vertical surface. Every day a little more soil falls from the top edge of the cliff; one day it will erode all the way back to the top of the hill, leaving our yard looking like a construction site.

The softest of all things
Overrides the hardest of all things.
                                (*Tao*, 43)

What can I do to save the life forms on and in the hill? Put up another wall? It's too expensive to hire a landscape contractor and I don't have the time to do the work myself. Bulldoze the whole backyard and level it? Way too expensive for us. Plant hedges in front of the cliff to block the construction site image? Possibly, but we already tried forsythia and it has not taken hold due to the loose dirt at the bottom of the cliff. But all this really does not address anything except the cosmetic issues, significant as these may be for our society.

*The Great Way is very smooth and straight;
And yet the people prefer devious paths.*
                                    (*Tao*, 53)

Well, the cliff itself is certainly fairly smooth and straight. But suburbanites prefer more devious paths to grace their backyards. So even though this eroding line of sight does not really bother me all that much, it does bother my wife a little and the neighbors a lot. ("Would you like some help fixin' that?" they ask.)

Nature is supposed to contain only curves, no Euclidean straight lines, but there are two exceptions: certain crystalline formations and my evenly eroding backyard cliff.

*What is well planted cannot be uprooted.
What is well embraced cannot slip away.
Your descendants will carry on the ancestral sacrifice for
    generations without end.*
                                    (*Tao*, 54)

I can only conclude that the backyard was not originally well-planted. Heaven forbid that my two grown children or their children would inherit this property and sacrifice their lives and fortunes to the unstoppable force of erosion.

A beautiful black locust tree, its long tap-root carrying nourishment upward against gravity, is also waging a losing battle against time in the backyard. So far, about a third of its root system has been exposed by the erosion. Only by my recent amputation of a few large limbs has the locust managed to stay alive, a green parasol over the right side of the cliff.

Clearly I have an unexpected ally here in the black locust. How can I use it to help me? How can I assist in its long-term survival, beyond the surgery I've already successfully performed?

*Therefore, the Sage [Wayfarer] squares without cutting,
carves without disfiguring,
straightens without straining,
enlightens without dazzling.*

(*Tao*, 58)

Most of the options I can think of sound like a lot of trouble. But another notion strikes me. What if I were to *increase* the erosion, somewhat expand it, deliberately cut the hill back further? Might that not expose some of the roots of the black locust and permit new locust trees to sprout from those roots? And wouldn't such sturdy new growth stop the erosion in its tracks?

The problems here are, first, that the roots may be too deep to encourage new little trees to grow from them. More serious is the slippery-slope argument: exposing too much of the tree's root system to the air might kill it, leaving nothing at all to slow the local forces of entropy.

But looking more broadly over "my" land, anti-erosion forces have indeed begun to make themselves felt, but in the front yard, not the back. The mound-building ants are still thriving. Could I just move the ant hills to the back yard and the erosion to the front?

Seriously, would I really want to have that much control over the environment? Control is a sensitive issue: each of us likes to control other persons and things but resents and resists *being* controlled by others.

The Bible apparently grants humans, who are said to have individual souls, control over all the flora and fauna of nature. "Dominion" is the old-fashioned word for control. A book entitled *Earth Might Be Fair* (edited by Ian Barbour; Prentice-Hall: 1972), which I assigned to students in my college classes two decades ago, argues that in Genesis, "stewardship" is a more appropriate translation than "dominion." In this modern interpretation, we humans have an ethical responsibility to preserve and protect flora and other fauna. We are their guardians, not their masters.

Hence, only he who is willing to give his body for the sake of the world is fit to be entrusted with the world. Only he who can do it with love is worthy of being the steward of the world.

(*Tao*, 13)

As in the non-traditional interpretation of Genesis, Taoism asks us to hold to this "feminine" or "yin" side of life. "Yang" is the masculine or aggressive half of these polarities.

*Know the masculine,
Keep to the feminine,
And be the Brook of the World.
To be the Brook of the World is
To move constantly in the path of Virtue
Without swerving from it,
And to return again to infancy.*

(*Tao*, 28)

Keep in mind that polarity is not the same as duality. An example of the latter is right vs. wrong: the dichotomy is mutually exclusive. Polarity, on the other hand, is exemplified by north and south - extremes that need each other and that eventually turn into and become the other. Or think of the difference between the modern scientific polarity of mass and energy vs. the ancient Aristotelian dualism of matter and form. Or perhaps it's better not to think about that, yet.

If you have ever read Carl Jung, you have seen polarities working at the very center of a profound psychological approach, one that seems to be gradually surpassing that of his mentor, Sigmund Freud, in its general impact. Whereas for Freud the conscious and the unconscious, for instance, are separate and distinct states of mind, for Jung they are polarities that complement each other and can even turn into the other. Jung felt the same way about *anima* and *animus*, the female and male principles in all of us. And Jung was explicit in crediting ancient Asian insights for the way he viewed these psychological matters.

Two Sides

The dominant European traditions, including Biblical roots, are dualistic: from Aristotle to Descartes, from grammar to law, from economics to politics, and from psychology to religion, the European universe divides into two incompatible parts: mind and matter, subject and object, supply and demand, the ruler and the governed, body and soul, good and evil, God and Nature...

Asian thinking, especially Chinese, tends toward polarity rather than duality. The *I Ching* or Book of Changes predates even Taoism and Buddhism: its teaching of the ultimate unity of yin and yang is at the heart of Chinese thought throughout its subsequent history. As Alan Watts says in his carefully worded way:

> *At the very roots of Chinese thinking and feeling there lies the principle of polarity, which is not to be confused with the ideas of opposition or conflict. In the metaphors of other cultures, light is at war with darkness, life with death, good with evil, and the positive with the negative, and thus an idealism to cultivate the former and be rid of the latter flourishes throughout much of the world. To the traditional way of Chinese thinking, this is as incomprehensible as an electric current without both positive and negative poles, for polarity is the principle that + and - , north and south, are different aspects of one and the same system, and that the disappearance of either one of them would be the disappearance of the system.*
> (*Tao: The Watercourse Way*; Pantheon: 1975, pp. 19-20)

The *Tao* continues that tradition and transforms it:

*All the myriad things carry the Yin on their backs and
hold the Yang in their embrace,
Deriving their vital harmony from the proper blending of
the two vital Breaths.*
(*Tao*, 42)

The Yin Side

Returning to the issue of control, we Westerners assume that nature - usually regarded as feminine - can and should be controlled, sometimes more, sometimes less. Otherwise we fear that our happiness and even our survival would be threatened. This helps to justify our economic ethic of constant competition. And until recently it has justified the pillaging of trees, meadows, wildlife, streams, and oceans.

Keeping to the yin side of things helps remind us that nature and other people can be influenced to our advantage and yet not be overcontrolled - by learning to use natural momentum:

*When the speed of rushing water reaches the point where
it can move boulders, this is the force of momentum.*
(*Sun Tzu*, p. 96)

But this yin approach takes patience and timing. Isn't the yang way more efficient? Why not just bring in the bulldozer to my backyard, throw pesticide on the front, and be done with it?

The answer is that yang is already too much with us. Total, overpowering control over nature is making human beings weaker. The mentality of warfaring - winning with raw technological force - ends up ultimately creating opposition from yin forces that really are beyond human control.

The pesticide strategy, for instance, would not merely kill birds, though that is a grievous loss when you multiply and generalize one suburbanite's action to all suburbanites' parallel actions everywhere.

Life is unimaginable without birds and, as I mentioned before, they may be all that stand between us and the uncountable insects some day!

Pesticides, if used by all or most suburbanites against ant-infestations, will dilute the power of natural chemicals and organisms in the soil and streams and oceans. These pesticides, used very broadly the way I am tempted to use them, will weaken - unleash too many yin forces upon - the agricultural and agronomic necessities of our human subsistence.

We must adopt a new environ-mentality or eco-logic, and

> *Therefore, the Sage [Wayfarer] embraces the One,*
> *And becomes a Pattern to all under Heaven.*
> (Tao, 22)

Meanwhile the bulldozer, even if I could afford it right now, is yang technology epitomized.

How could it ever lead to yin excess? Easily - by crushing and smashing the roots of the one living thing, that single black locust on the edge of the cliff, which is holding back complete and final erosion. The locust is doing that by actually holding the entire hill together as one cohesive dirt-web of life.

With crushed roots there would be no locust tree; without that tree - no hill to be held together.

Therefore the bulldozer solution means eradication of the hill itself. Yet the very goal I had in the first place was preservation of the life in and on that hill. Death is the final word of yin.

Richard Spiegel

As Ssu-K'ung T'u, the last of the great Tang poets, says:

Expenditure of force leads to outward decay,
Spiritual existence means inward fullness.
Let us revert to Nothing and enter the Absolute,
Hoarding up strength for Energy.
Freighted with eternal principles,
Athwart the mighty void ...
Beyond the range of conceptions,
Let us gain the Centre,
And there hold fast without violence,
Fed from an inexhaustible supply.
   (from *Taoist Tales*, edited by Raymond Van Over;
                          Mentor: 1973, p. 231)

As we will see later on, this "center" or pivot is no mystical abstraction.

"The World is a Sacred Vessel"

"Virtual" Reality

I am mowing the lawn, and now taking a break and sitting on the wooden deck in my backyard. It is the only level area at the rear of the house. From here the hill goes up at a steep angle for 25 feet, then comes the three-foot-high mini-cliff of eroding earth with plant roots exposed all along the top of the 50-foot wide ledge. Between the deck and the cliff are a few scattered wild flowers, rose bushes (Carolina and hybrid tea), thirteen of them deep pink, irises that have not come up this year, a very few daffodils, and weeds. I always cut and do not pull out the humble weeds.

Above our hill the terrain continues upward. All around the edge of the back of our property are trees, mostly elm, oak, dogwood, maple, black locust (of course), and shrubs and saplings. Two spread-out, bluish-green-gray Eastern White Pines guard either side. In the far upper right quadrant, along a dense copse of locust, hundreds of wild daylilies have recently and suddenly bloomed, new orange blossoms quietly replacing fading flowers, such that the whole collection appears unchanging even as individuals come and go. Between me and the daylilies sits Jack, our brand-new Rottweiler puppy.

Speaking of individuals: a year ago I myself planted a young Crape Myrtle, which I always just called "Myrtle," in the middle of the front yard (also a downward hill). At the time I didn't know anything about watering young trees, so poor Myrtle passed on. That's another reason why this black locust in the backyard is so important to me... it redeems me.

Today it is mostly cloudy and cool with a strong erratic breeze coming out of the east, through the maples and dogwoods and then past the black locust. We call these "easterlies," but in the old days they called them "westerlies," based on the direction not the source. Again I think of Columbus, who was able to find the right winds to take him to the New World, then tapped into the prevailing trade winds to get home.

That ability to intuit direction, to orienteer on the high seas though definitely not on land, was Columbus' greatest "Virtue" or "*Teh*" - as in *Tao Teh Ching*. This is true whether we esteem or decry him or his first contacts with the New World, or even how we value or evaluate the later consequences of his "discovery" of this world... our world.

One manifestation of this *Teh* was his conviction that he had to sail west in order to get to India (the "Indies") or China ("Cathay"), which of course were and are east of Europe. Even though all semi-educated sailors of the era knew the world was round, they had no idea of the true size of the globe.

> *The world is a sacred vessel, which must not be tampered with or grabbed after.*
> *To tamper with it is to spoil it, and to grasp it is to lose it.*
> (*Tao*, 29)

Picture the Earth as a convex vessel. It is the empty spaces of a vessel that are its greatest value. It is the null areas that have all the potential. On the convex surface of the Earth are low, concave areas that the oceans have filled up. Life probably originated in these lowest, most receding spots. And they have the greatest potential for benefit or harm to the life still on Earth.

This potential, this power, is Virtue or *Teh*. All yin or "empty" spaces are symbolically filled with it. The word "Virtue" with a capital "V" is used here in its old-fashioned sense: for instance, the Virtue of the ginseng root is its power to slow down or offset aging, according to ancient Asian teaching. This concept of Virtue is one of power rather than morality. In both the Chinese and European cultures the morally neutral conception of Virtue as power gradually became a moral notion ("virtuous") under the influence of Confucianism in the East and Christianity in the West.

Both senses of "virtue" are subtly captured, one in the title and another in the body of an ancient Taoist story, "The Virtue of Meekness":

> *Opening his mouth so as to show his tongue, Chang Ts'ung asked Lao Tzu, "Is my tongue still there?"*
> *"Yes."*
> *"Are my teeth also intact then?"*
> *"No, they are gone."*
> *"The tongue is preserved by reason of its softness, while the teeth are destroyed owing to their hardness. Is that not so?"*
> *Chang Ts'ung nodded in assent.*
> (Raymond Van Over, ed., *Taoist Tales]*)

The moral virtue of meekness (or, as we will see, humility) contrasts with the natural, nonmoral power inherent in softness and hardness in this Eastern parable.

Robert M. Pirsig, in *Zen and the Art of Motorcycle Maintenance* (William Morrow: 1974), clarifies for us the first *Western* thinkers who tried to preserve Virtue as power rather than as morality: the much-despised Sophists of ancient Greece. Their phrase was "arete," excellence: the potential of a great athlete to win a race, or the power of a natural orator to lead a nation. This is *Teh*.

> *Thirty spokes converge upon a single hub;*
> *It is on the hole in the center that the use of the cart hinges.*
> *We make a vessel from a lump of clay;*

> It is the empty space within the vessel that makes it useful.
>
> (*Tao*, 11)

The *Tao Teh Ching* itself is an empty vessel. Its many translations into English tend to reflect the culture and era of the translator. In the 1980s, for instance, R. L. Wing's rendition, called *The Tao of Power* (Dolphin: 1986), brought in nuances of "power" not in the sense that I am using it but as in "control." For this is what the yuppie readers of the fast-track Eighties wanted to hear. Before that, a beautiful and poetic translation by Gia-fu Feng and Jane English (Vintage: 1972) emphasized peace-and-love themes and mysticism. The translation I cite here - John C. H. Wu's - is both unembellished and sensitively phrased, no doubt reflecting its mid-20th century milieu.

Many Westerners who would like to be Sages or Wayfarers nevertheless find such openness and ambivalence unnerving.

They want a "correct" or definitive translation. But they forget that in their own tradition there are Catholic Bibles, Protestant Bibles, fundamentalist translations, liberal interpretations, and orthodox exegeses. The Taoist "bible" is similarly open to many but not all possible interpretations, just as any major cultural vessel (or holy grail) must be.

The *Tao* even has its own version of the Dead Sea Scrolls. In 1973, two silk manuscripts, called the Ma-wang-tui texts after the name of the location, were discovered in central China. five hundred years older than other translations, the Ma-wang-tui manuscripts have influenced some recent translators; an example is Victor H. Mair (Bantam: 1990) who renders "*Teh*" as "integrity," an odd but intriguing suggestion, as we will see. Integrity is the power of connectedness, of being whole by being part of a whole, by being rooted. Wu's way of putting this point:

> *Attain to utmost Emptiness.*
> *Cling single-heartedly to interior peace.*
> *While all things are stirring together,*
> *I only contemplate the Return.*
> *For flourishing as they do,*
> *Each of them will return to its root.*
> <div align="right">(<i>Tao</i>, 16)</div>

By the Light of Teh

All of this leads or rather returns me to my hill. Perhaps I should begin to view this open area between the deck and the cliff as emptiness, as potential, as power on the yin side. With the lawn freshly mowed all around it, it does have the appearance of a vessel. It is an elongated, almost elliptical bowl-shape rimmed distinctly on the two long sides and vaguely on the ends. I seem to have before me no longer a mere problem but also an opportunity, a microcosm of *Teh*, potentiality. Whether it ends up as a "good" or "bad" space depends on what I do or do not make of it.

> *The Tao is like an empty bowl,*
> *Which in being used can never be filled up.*
> *Fathomless, it seems to be the origin of all things.*
> <div align="right">(<i>Tao</i>, 4)</div>

It's good I finished mowing: the easterly wind may be bringing a storm through any time now. As the leaves shake and twist I perceive and count at least fifteen hues of green. A couple of trees are almost blue, their green is that deep.

But I need to turn my attention away from green leaves and toward green dollars. Soon I must go back to work. I am a fundraiser, a high-stress yang job if there ever was one. The nonprofit organizations I have worked for (and I have raised many millions for them over the years) need all the help they can get. It seems like this leaves little or no room for yin in this all-too-typical business situation. Yang means competitiveness, among other things, and that's what contemporary fundraising is all about. The economics of downsizing, an increased number of nonprofit organizations, the reduced number of giving sources due to all the buyouts and mergers of the last decade, and the growing professionalization of corporate contributions and foundation grantmaking staffs - all these have brought out the yang in development people.

Yet there are ways to remember the yin, even in fundraising:

The Way means inducing the people to have the same aim as the leadership, so that they will share death and share life, without fear of danger.
(*Sun Tzu*, p. 43)

Harmony of purpose in a business organization of any kind is unusually important for success in the market place. But to harmonize is not to insist on one tune; indeed, harmony requires many simultaneous voices. It is up to the leadership to create the single purpose or mission that harmonizes all the disparate voices. This is leadership in its yin mode.

The perception of eye and ear are not sufficient to distinguish the inner designs of things; intellectual discourse is not sufficient to determine right and wrong. Those who use their wits to govern have a hard time maintaining a nation; only those who realize universal harmony and keep to spontaneous response can do it.
(*Huainanzi*, p. 46)

Whether in a nation, a business or a nonprofit group, we must implement pursuit of the mission with joy but without every detail planned out. Once the aims are yang-clear, yin flexibility and spontaneity keep things creative. Macro-management not micro-management fits with Taoism.

> *If you want to know the way of the sky, observe the seasonal cycles. If you want to know the way of the earth, find out what kind of trees grow there. If you want to know the way of people, let them have what they want.*
> (*Huainanzi*, p. 26)

For some Taoist wisdom about modern fundraising in particular, just substitute "donors" for "people" in the last sentence. No better advice can be given.

Modern marketing often begins with a typically yang approach to organizational goal-setting: here are the objectives for the year, these are the main marketing strategies for achieving the objectives, and those are the specific market results (outcomes) to be produced and the evaluation tools to be applied to test those results.

A more yin approach would be to begin not with one's own objectives or ambitions but with the customer's: what and where is the market demand for our product among specific constituencies and how can the product best be delivered to them? The organization's objectives will be the answers to those questions.

Two more yin contributions to contemporary business are the roles of intuition, which we will examine later on, and patience, which we will look at right now. Intuition requires patience:

> *Even wise leaders must await appropriate circumstances. Appropriate circumstances can only be found at the right time and cannot be fulfilled through being sought by knowledge.*
> (*Huainanzi*, p. 3)

All very successful business people know that timing is the key to success and timing is not a matter for the intellect but for intuition. And that comes to us when it's good and ready.

Success is a matter of timing, not contention.
(Huainanzi, p. 77)

Reaching harmony for the "business" self is the opposite of egoism, which occurs when one economic mask or role overpowers and unbalances other personae. To recognize any state of harmony - the poised tension of apparent "opposite" roles - one must also recognize and include (or attract) various "extremes" to balance our roles. For example, if your boss is too aggressive toward you, show him the Virtue of your quiet diplomatic skills. If a co-worker is jealous of your track record, invite her to join you in your successes.

Feeling intuitively is like cultivating the earth; planning intellectually is like planting grass seeds in that earth. You can be the most aggressive sower, but if you don't patiently cultivate the soil and instinctively sense (have a hunch) when it is most receptive, most of your seeds will lie fallow forever.

Although the *Tao* and I emphasize the place of yin, we do so only to help counter the dominance of yang in so many cultures. But over and over in this book it will be made clear that it is the *balance*, the harmony, the unity of all apparent "opposites," that counts. Yin traits can be taken too far as well, so far that they will generate their own yang counterparts - just as yang characteristics that are not counterbalanced by equal yin will eventually breed their own type of yin consequences.

There can never be too much yin or too much yang as long as they balance each other. For Taoism it is not the extreme state but the unbalanced state that throws things off track... and off the Way.

I can see an amazing example of too much yang without the compensating yin right now - a big Bradford Pear tree on the street alongside my neighbor's sidewalk.

This neighbor kept trimming this stately, up-reaching ornamental until it artificially acquired the shape (no, not of a pear) of an ice-cream cone: a perfect fat cone, no branches at all at the bottom, smooth as silk on the sides, peaked on top.

So, naturally, over the last few months three separate and vicious gusts of wind have snapped off its three largest, most graceful branches. The perfect geometrical shape provides lift, just as with an airplane wing. The main branches must have been pulled up and out, their own gravity then snapping them back down with equal and opposite force. Now the neighbor says he will have to cut down the poor pear tree. It will die for his sins.

With nature and in the office, each of us has to find and recognize the most effective, productive balance of yang aggressiveness and yin receptivity. It is true that American business tends to financially reward yang traits over yin, but because too much of one trait always leads to its complement, that economic convenience cannot last forever.

We already are seeing "creativity" financially valued in high-tech computer businesses, especially software companies paving the Information Highway, with its new loops, filling stations, data restaurants, entrance ramps and exits, maps and guides constantly coming into and going out of existence.

With this proactive approach to harmonizing yin and yang in mind, let's look back at the front lawn I just finished mowing. The faster, the thicker and the higher the grass grows, the more often it has to be cut down. The balance of yang growth and yin mowing is the key to my stewardship of the lawn, and its sign.

I for one want a slow luxuriant growth. These anthills are neither. Their net perceptible effect goes too far in the direction of yin no-growth. Things of the lawn kind are out of harmony. One form of life (the ants) grows relatively faster than another, at least equally valuable form (the grass). As a result, the yang of the ants leads to its opposite, the sparse yin-decline and perhaps the eventual death of the grass.

I arrive at the same conclusion concerning the erosion in the backyard, except as a mirror image. The overpowering yin that is eroding the potential yang-life in and on my backyard is producing imbalances that, left to themselves, will be resolved only by the most unpredictable of consequences. And aside from their ultimate consequences or even their complex causes, the disharmonies of both the front and the back are becoming visibly ugly.

Natural beauty, though not the only kind, is our paradigm of beauty as harmony. As natural beings, much less as Wayfarers, we need harmony inside us before we can truly recognize the beauty external to ourselves. Whether in the office or on the lawn, the natural principles are the same: we must value, recognize and incorporate the balancing polarities that make us whole, people of integrity, regardless of society's likely evaluation of us as excessive or deficient.

Maybe this is what Hemingway had in mind when he says, at the end of *Death in the Afternoon*, that "any part you make will represent the whole if it's made truly."

Aristotle's Child

A Question of Balance

Up to this point, my Wayfaring has focused on helping to rebalance the world that appears external to me. Now the *Tao* requires me to rebalance my own internal universe, the lawn of my mind, as well.

There are two very different meaning of "balance." The classical Greek (Western) ideal, suggested by Plato but really developed by his star pupil, Aristotle, is to find the mean or midpoint between any two extremes. This concept of moderation was the basis of both the dominant Greek ideal of what is "just" and, across the Christian era, the prevailing European concept of what is "virtuous."

As the paradigm of "fairness" in its various meanings, the concept of justice applied originally to associations of persons, such as the state, and only derivatively to those persons as individuals. Conversely, as the paradigm of "goodness," the concept of virtue (with a small "v") applied first and foremost to individuals, secondarily to states, societies and other groupings. Justice is the macro-concept, virtue the micro-concept.

In the Aristotelian-Christian tradition, the one most of us were born into, the great evil is extremism, that is, lack of moderation and loss of control to "excess." A "balanced" person, psychologically, avoids extremes of anger or passion or sensuality; a balanced society educates its members to respect moderation in verbal, physical, and artistic expression and even in knowledge itself. A balanced or just state is governed moderately, by virtuous individuals with moderate cultural values. Such a state would represent a middle point between two excesses.

Contemporary post-industrial capitalism, for instance,

is thought to represent a midpoint somewhere between old-fashioned 19th-century dog-eat-dog capitalism and the socialist/communist ideal of non-competitiveness and equal distribution of economic goods and social services.

Now think back to your childhood: there was always another child who could ride the seesaw by himself or herself. That child had enough of a sense of physical and tactile balance to be able to stand over the fulcrum of the seesaw and find the shifting middle point between the two extremes.

That, basically, is Aristotle's ideal of balance through moderation: the ethical doctrine is analogous to the ideal Greek geometry, the "golden mean." More exactly, moderate individuals, under conditions we will take a look at later, become virtuous; and when enough virtuous people have political and police powers, the whole city/state is automatically a just one. And the perfect leader represents moderation so well that, like that little child you envied so long ago, he can always sense the best middle course for the society or state. (The latter are conceptual constructs that are kept separate nowadays but were more or less the same in Plato's and Aristotle's time, three to four centuries B.C.)

Plato was open to a second concept of balance, one that might not only include more than two extremes, but even more importantly, might not include moderation at all! For example, again speaking psychologically, a born leader might represent in himself a balance of intellectual gifts over emotions as well as over appetites like hunger; a born fighter's or soldier's passions, particularly courage, would outweigh the power of his intellect or sexual drive; a farmer might be driven more to growing and eating good food than to either reading books or going off to war.

In Plato's second ideal of balance, embodied in much of the *Republic*, everyone would be in their proper, productive place, and justice would then prevail on both the individual and societal levels.

But after Aristotle and his focus on moderation in all

things, Greek values, followed later by Roman and then medieval Christian ideals, held that justice was balance and balance was the midpoint between any and all dichotomies: justice became as dualistic as any other Western ideal. Moderation between two extremes became the essence of both justice and moral virtue.

However, every once in a while, Europeans in great numbers historically hark back to Plato, leapfrogging over Aristotle, as the artists of the Renaissance did. But the seeds of immoderation in Plato's thought are always drowned out by the Aristotelians, who have normally controlled Western philosophy and religion. Some of these seeds came from even earlier philosophers, pre-Socratics like Heraclitus and Empedocles, who began Western cosmological thinking. For Empedocles, for instance, Love (attraction) and Strife (repulsion) balance out but do not compromise one another.

Seesawing

Yet, when you were a child playing with a friend on the seesaw at the playground, together you represented an alternative concept to the balancing-act of Aristotle's child - that lone child on the other seesaw. On your own seesaw you were on one end, your friend was on the other, no one at all was in the middle. The two extremes balanced each other (except, of course, when a much heavier child or big parent would take the other end, plop it down hard and leave you perched high up). This twosome is another view of balance, of harmony, not as avoiding extremes but rather as taking advantage of them - using them to your benefit: "counterbalancing."

We can see this tendency toward justice, as counterbalancing but not diluting extremes, by taking the approach to mental health that Plato would likely do if he were alive today. With him, psychological health lies not in moderation per Aristotle, but in all our "extremes" balancing one another: equilibrium maintained, for instance, not by never getting furious at a rival in the workplace but by balancing that great anger with deep empathy for her current hurt feelings or with thoughtful sensitivity to her past troubled background.

In contrast, in balancing-by-moderation, the weight (thought, passion, or desire) is in the middle of the two possible extremes of too much and too little (technically, excess and deficiency). In counterbalancing, on the other hand, the weight is equal at both ends of the spectrum; and if not, it is as valid to add more to one end as it is to subtract from the other.

While moderation became the heart of Western morality, the archetype of counterbalance is still culturally preserved in the ancient Chaldean mystic symbol of justice - the scales that "Lady Justice" blindly holds to balance guilt and punishment precisely and equitably. And the Chaldean, non-Aristotelian concept of justice does live on in many ordinary Americans' view of criminal justice as providing punishment that is precisely as extreme as the crime, and their resistance to being moderate in meting out punishment for a crime.

The latter would be compatible with the generally prevailing concept of justice as fairness - in the workplace, in personal relationships, in the whole cosmos - but it does not satisfy "an eye for an eye," or justice as retribution. This idea is not Aristotelian, rather out of our Judeo-Christian heritage.

Independently (one presumes) of all these Western developments, the Taoists in the Orient also pursued the concept of counterbalance, or balance as harmony, by retaining or achieving equal extremes or "opposites." The two children at each end of the seesaw need each other to play; along the same lines, on the "macro" level,

The Huainan masters speak of healthy societies in terms of balance and harmony on each level of being, from the

way the individual human body-mind complex experiences itself to the way it experiences interaction with the natural and social worlds.
(Thomas Cleary in his Introduction to *The Tao of Politics*, viii)

So, processing all this through my own experience, my harmony may lie in the Platonist/Taoist sense of counterbalancing extreme tendencies and not in the Aristotelian sense of doing and feeling "nothing in excess." And I personally need to understand what this possibility means, first for my own psychological micro-life and then for coping with the macro-necessities of social life. Surely these are essential to know before I can tell where the balance lies between the anthills and grass in the front yard or between the erosion and plant growth in the back. If the seesaw I'm riding is not steady, I can't notice whether other seesaws around me are balanced either.

Aristotle's child keeps the seesaw more or less level but all his energy goes into keeping the seesaw as still as possible - otherwise he will fall off. A Taoist child, along with his required partner or partners, produces much more dynamic, up-and-down motion. The greater momentum of the Taoist child generates in him awareness of constant change and of his dependence on other living things; but it also produces its own threat of instability.

As to my own potential, my current momentum, my *Teh*: my Virtue in the sense of personal power is greater, though my virtue in the sense of traditional moral correctness may not be, as I seek to preserve and understand and utilize the extremes of my feelings, thoughts and actions. In fact, my Virtue might very well grow out of such extremes when they harmonize with each other. Once I am more confident that I am personally and socially in counterbalance - a whole and complete person, a man of integrity - I can be a better judge of what other living things might need for their own balancing acts.

Cultivate Virtue in your own person,
And it becomes a genuine part of you.
Cultivate it in the family,
And it will abide.
Cultivate it in the community,
And it will live and grow.
Cultivate it in the state,
And it will flourish abundantly.
Cultivate it in the world,
And it will become universal.

Hence, a person must be judged as person;
A family as family;
A community as community;
A state as state;
The world as world.
How do I know about the world?
By what is within me.
                              (Tao, 54)

These lines also make me think of the way Chamfort described passions: "it is only because they exaggerate that they are passions."

I have always wanted to avoid being mediocre. Now I am just beginning to understand what the price (and the value) of that goal might really be.

Carry the Yin, Embrace the Yang

Wu Wei

As the time approaches for making decisions - knowing I have to take firm action that will affect other lives - practical ethics moves gradually to the foreground, other and more speculative issues to the background, of my life's picture. This is true whether I work on my yard or my life.

First the yard: whether I choose to poison other people and fish with pesticides I spread over the anthills, or to kill the ants themselves as well as local birds; whether I destroy the black locust or just inflict a lot of noise and commotion or even apathy on my neighbors, I cannot avoid having an impact on other living things.

The key Chinese sign in Taoist ethics is *wu wei*, or the full ideogram, *wei wu wei* - not-doing, noninterference, nonaction, or sometimes, noncooperation: to do by not-doing. In the translation I am using, the awkward English phrase is "non-ado." But in fact there is no exact and accurate English rendering for *wu wei*. Perhaps most often noninterference or nonintervention best captures the ethical notion:

> *The softest of all things*
> *Overrides the hardest of all things.*
> *Only Nothing can enter into no-space.*
> *Hence I know the advantages of Non-Ado*
> *[noninterference].*
> (*Tao*, 43)

Taoist art - internationally renowned as the Way of the Uncarved Block - expresses *wu wei* in its endless convolutions, continuous organic form, soft welcoming textures, and use of objects found in their natural state. In our Western artistic tradition, Michelangelo claimed that he did not create sculptures, but just removed or chipped away the stone to reveal the form that exists independently of the artist. This is Platonist and Taoist at the same time. But *wu wei* is even more subtle when applied to ethics:

> *Do the Non-Ado [Do by not-doing].*
> *Strive for the effortless.*
> *Savour the savourless.*
> *Exalt the low.*
> *Multiply the few.*
> *Requite injury with kindness.*
>
> *Nip troubles in the bud.*
> *Sow the great in the small.*
>
> *Difficult things of the world*
> *Can only be tackled when they are easy.*
> *Big things of the world*
> *Can only be achieved by attending to their small*
>   *beginnings.*
> *Thus, the Sage [Wayfarer] never has to grapple with big*
>   *things,*
> *Yet he alone is capable of achieving them!*
>
> (*Tao*, 63)

To my surprise, it appears that Chapter 63 would have had me act sooner and more decisively on my lawn problems... on their "small beginnings." That would have encouraged use of minimum force on - less interference in - the "natural" ways of anthill building and back-hill erosion. By now, these problems are "big things" to me. It is much harder to alter things now without bringing in the heavy artillery of pesticides and bulldozers.

So *wu wei* is not passivity; it is not advocating a do-nothing attitude. Often, to minimize interference with nature - to find the lawn's way - one has to act fast and decisively.

Of course, as a modern or post-modern suburban American, I have already compromised myself. I certainly interfere with nature or what's left of nature or what's left of it between the houses and the driveways. But I did not choose or create modern technological culture, though I take full advantage of it and also accept its disadvantages.

Given my involvement, my cultural reality, what is the least intrusive, least unnatural way to deal with my little anthills and my big eroding hill? Again, I might need to act very aggressively in order to grab any remaining opportunities in time to offer minimal interference in what I had always assumed were two different sets of problems with two separate yards, back and front.

In Taoism, an option in decision-making is defined as what lies in my control. Although there always seems to be another option, the latter is not always what it may at first seem to be. I need to recognize those actions that I can actually execute. For much less in the world is under my control than I like to believe.

I can help or slow the growth or the grass but I cannot influence the rain. I can somewhat alter the nutrient content of the soil but not whether it was originally sand or clay or loam.

Just as we have seen how detrimental it is to try to over-control nature, we have even less control over other people - and Taoism includes people as part of nature. It does appear to us that we show our children what sort of persons they ought to be, give orders to subordinates, make relatives feel guilty, and otherwise manipulate others' behavior to our own ends.

Actually, such people only like to give us the impression that they are really changing: their overt behavior, what is obvious and visible, briefly changes even though their inner desires, needs, and values do not usually change. Complex organisms are more than the sum of their visible behaviors.

In terms already explained, the inner life is the hidden or yin side; the whole person is not changed unless this side of her or him also alters. Overt behavior is just one aspect of the whole being.

> All the myriad things carry the Yin on their backs and
> hold the Yang in their embrace,
> Deriving their vital harmony from the proper blending of
> the two vital Breaths.
>
> (*Tao*, 42)

I am the agent of harmony wherever and whenever I am truly effective. My Western culture happens to revere the yang: the masculine, the aggressive, the explicit, the overt, the independent. So to harmonize with my social reality I cannot ignore yang solutions in favor of a one-sided understanding of *wu wei*.

What to Do?

Two issues require ethical resolution: what is needed to redress the imbalances in nature (backyard downsizing, front-yard takeover); and what is required for me to personally maintain my always-tenuous equilibrium with my society, especially as I attempt to mitigate the first issue... harmony in nature implies harmony of nurture.

At first it strikes me that the societal issue may be nothing more than a problem of social perception. Perhaps I only need to neutralize the lawn problem to the point (no more and no less) where my neighbors and visitors and local authorities no longer perceive or notice the ant infestation or the hill erosion. Can I just handle these issues cosmetically?

If changing others' perceptions means they no longer see a problem when they look at my yard, then perhaps I should just fence in or plant high hedges around all of my property... but that would cost more money than real solutions would.

There is a more important reason not to go with the cosmetic response, and that is my genuine responsibility to do something to protect the growth potential - the *Teh* - of the grass out front and of the burgeoning foliage in back. Simply put, the anthills must not be allowed to snuff out all the other, very beautiful growth; and the erosion cannot be permitted to slowly kill the black locust and every other green plant, shrub and flower - including, by the way, the daylilies that are spreading their orangeness over more and more of the right side of the backyard.

Is there a yin-based solution to all this? I just read in the newspaper about a local company in Virginia that is developing a nontoxic biopesticide derived from natural sugar. But it is not yet approved for public use.

In the meantime, for all the reasons I discussed, I can use the garden hose to wash away the anthills regularly and to encourage the growth of the new grass. Yet I know that this very yin approach is ultimately futile, a new Myth of Sisyphus for the suburbs, and ultimately a waste of water and of my time.

I am aware that Lao Tzu would not have worried about wasting time; even Lewis Carroll made fun of the Western obsession with time when he had the Mad Hatter advise Alice in Wonderland to stop beating Time when she learned music and to keep on good terms with Time. On the other hand, it is unlikely that either Lao Tzu or Lewis Carroll worried about wasting water either.

Meanwhile, the black locust suggests a parallel, least-intrusive response to the erosion in the backyard. I could plant new junipers or yews all along the ledge-top; perhaps someday they would hold the soil together and creep over the edge, then down the cliff to hide it.

Having carried the yin solutions on my back this far, I see that I would not be very satisfied with such weak responses, either directly to the yard issues or indirectly to society's expectations. While bulldozers and toxins bring on too much yang, nevertheless all this yin thinking needs some yang concepts to balance it off.

In Taoism, "power" in the yang sense of controlling other persons or other living things can never be the goal of our conduct because "power" in the yin sense - Virtue or potentiality - is that goal. But can raw, Westernized power as forcefulness or control be utilized as a temporary means to rebalancing or counterbalancing ourselves or other beings?

Clearly the answer for modern Western Wayfarers has to be a qualified Yes. Yang power, always used as a means and never solely as an end, can and must sometimes be tapped into to rectify overbalancing yin forces. Erosion of the yard and of my everyday relationship with society - both of which have to be intact in order to serve as protection - are obvious cases of too much yin.

This revision of the Kantian categorical imperative - which, as we will see, states that we must treat people as ends, as intrinsically valuable, and never solely as instruments for our own purposes - prohibits the use of force except as a means to greater balance. This occasional exception is also an exception to *wu wei*: though doing by not-doing is the Taoist rule of thumb, sometimes we have to do-by-doing; sometimes we have to forcefully intervene with nature.

In the Way

I'm beginning to see that the tension inherent in the equilibrium between extremes is the momentum, the stored energy that is *Teh*.

Turning now, with reluctance, to my own interactions with my neighbors and the larger society around me, I could certainly choose to simply cover up the unsightly cliff and even keep washing away anthill after anthill, but those responses would not really put me in harmony or back in balance with human observers. Although I still have to use minimum force, yang may be required as much for my interpersonal landscape as for fixing the front and back lawns.

And the longer I wait to address any of my disharmonies with my society, the more out of balance things will get. Yang decisiveness is required on both levels, the lawn and myself. In fact, I may have a personal front-yard issue and a personal backyard issue that may be preventing me from making "virtuous decisions" (in *both* the Eastern and the Western senses) even about the lawn.

I realize, first, that I do tend to build my own innumerable anthills, which slow my own personal growth. I keep trying, in a way that is obviously futile in the eyes of the rest of the world, to wash away episodes of frustration after frustration, but they keep coming back.

These anthills of personal frustration are my accumulated resentments against the social demands on my time.

Time...

I have never really adapted to the fact that society structures almost all of my time for me. About 14 hours a day going to and from work, including dressing and undressing, commuting and fundraising activities; about one hour with neighbors, bill collectors and providers of so-called services; add to these 15 hours one more for eating, five for sleeping (that's all I need) and one for recovering from exhaustion due to all the other mandated activities... and I am left with no more than two hours a day of living-time. I resent that and always have.

I am incapable, I admit, of not working hard or long hours; when I work I am very yang, very compulsive about working. But I would prefer not to have to work for others at all.

So you see, this is why I have taken off this summer, my first summer off since I was a college teacher many years ago, when I taught philosophy in Wisconsin. I recently resigned from one fundraising position and have been interviewing for others in hopes of finding more happiness.

Thinking back into time, being a young professor of philosophy was an easy way to be with time, with the passing moments. Too bad I had to get bored with academia, because the ivory tower - though a prison or protection from the harsh ordinary world - does allow you to structure your own day more than other jobs do.

I suppose many people would say that it is mortality, my own death, and not an abstract dimension, that obsesses me. Yet I am not aware of having ever been terribly afraid of death. Death of people close to me has always been a familiar sight.

Still, my awareness of time, the passing of time, never leaves me when I am at work. Only out here in my yard or otherwise immersed in nature do I lose my sense that time is running out. Stillness is not with me away from nature.

How to become an urban Wayfarer? The ant heaps of time build up only on soil not well cultivated with serenity.

I need to see the time problem together and in balance with my *space* problem. The erosion in my backyard is also the eroding space of my existence. I always feel that modern America is too crowded, too polluted, that each day I lose a little more breathing room. And my loss of space is someone else's financial gain - more real estate or another parking lot.

The late California poet, Robinson Jeffers, noticed his

beloved space, "Carmel Point," being overrun by development and by people. Yet he can see that

*It has all time. It knows
the people are a tide
That swells and in time will ebb, and all
Their works dissolve...*

In fact this was why I left Southern California some time ago: no more space. Talk about erosion! The whole L.A. basin is eroding away as trees become luxuries and thin green lines against intruders. L.A. is now the symbol of erosion of space, for it once was a paradise of elbow room, of spaciousness, of endless mountains, canyons, deserts, orchards, and rivers. Now, if it were not for all the Hispanic gardeners and migrant agricultural workers, Southern California would (and still might) erode into the Pacific Ocean on a very rainy day or the day of the Big One - the predicted earthquake registering 8.0 or more on the Richter Scale.

But even here, in more stable Maryland, I have problems related to my sense of spatial erosion. One neighbor, way above us on the top of our mutual hill, has been blasting away at renegade weeds with an internal-combustion contraption. Another neighbor, a teenager, has been regularly taking a short-cut across the right side of our yards, along the wall of orange daylilies. Still another neighbor wants to make extended small talk whenever he gets me in his sights. Meanwhile airplanes swoop low to land in Baltimore. Stereos occasionally blare. Dogs bark intermittently and sharply. And all this in a neighborhood quieter than most.

Yet the single black locust tree in my backyard is doing more for it than I am doing for my own sense of eroding space. My vacation from work may just be avoidance of my cosmic issues of space as well as time. That may indicate that my attitude up to now has carried too much yin.

Back in the '70s, when I was teaching philosophy, I

used to assign readings from the works of Jacob Needleman, a philosopher of religion. In addition to the reference I already made to his interest in Taoist "metaphysical ethics," Needleman published a book, *Money and the Meaning of Life*, a meditation on the reality of how, in modern life, money is intertwined with all of our highest values. On the issue of how we fit in with our concepts of time and space he asks:

> *Why has time disappeared in our culture? How is it that after decades of inventions and new technologies devoted to saving time and labor, the result is that there is no time left? We are a time-poor society; we are temporally impoverished. And there is no issue, no aspect of human life, that exceeds this in importance. The destruction of time is literally the destruction of life...*
>
> *... If we are going to find a new approach to the money question, it will have to enable us to bring time back into our lives.*
>
> *As with time, so with space... This absence of personal space is the visual symbol of what the wisdom teachings of all ages have referred to as the condition of self-identification with one's desires and fears. In the East this is called "attachment." In the West it has been called, simply, "capture."*
>
> (Doubleday: 1991, pp. 29-30)

A more yang approach comes from Fan Yunqiao, a third-century A.D. Taoist poet:

> *What's the need to bow and pray*
> *To beg for long life?*
> *Clearly the original spirit*
> *Is thoroughly pure.*
> *Shatter space to become completely free...*
>   (IS, pp. 72-73)

This is exactly where many contemporary searchers bog down. Poetic philosophy or philosophical poetry sounds great, but there is no clear way to bring it down to earth. "Shatter space"? Here is the translator's note on this expression:

> To "shatter space" is the final step of a traditional progression of Taoist practice: refine vitality into energy, refine energy into spirit, refine spirit into space, shatter space to merge with the Tao.
>
> (IS, p. 73)

Refining my life force (*vitality*) has stalled at the point where spirit unites with my spatial perceptions, and apparently I cannot break away from being captured by the latter without first freeing myself from my obsession with time passing me by... from the poverty of modern time.

So to shatter space I must either first shatter time and the shackles of my traditional Western assumptions about what time is, or come up with a unification of spatial with temporal dimensions that puts me at peace with my life. These yang alternatives might even turn out to be one and the same action... perhaps space and time themselves will turn into one and the same reality.

When you shatter something, you can either break it apart for good or recombine it with something else. And remember how Robinson Jeffers' grief over losing precious natural space (and beauty) seemed soothed by its relationship to time. This is a poetic intuition about how we can see the physical world.

On the Way

Faces of Time

Of all the Ways that have come to light, none so radically challenged Western concepts of space and time as ancient Maya philosophy/science. The European conquerors systematically extirpated the Maya written libraries of philosophy treatises, histories of their gods, astronomical predictions, mathematical computations of cosmic time (utilizing zero and millions as arithmetic tools long before Europeans did), and calendars far more accurate than anything the West invented until very recently. The original peoples in and around the Yucatan Peninsula offered a theoretical and practical alternative to the space and time you and I know.

To comprehend this alternative way of thinking and perceiving, let's not analyze space as a "thing" vs. time as a "thing" or entity - even if our European languages do regard "them" as nouns.

Such "reification" of symbolic words into actual reality must be questioned if Maya concepts of total reality are to be partially understood and assimilated by today's Wayfarers.

So let us instead look at Maya time and then Maya spacetime. A few writings and other records escaped the Church's attempt to root out apparently devilish challenges to Christianity and its financially rewarding support of the gold- and silver-crazed soldiers from across the eastern sea. These remaining written and graphic records were inscribed in codes that were broken only a few decades ago, so the "metaphysical" view presented below is just one way of looking at Maya time.

On this Maya view of time, I will quote extensively from Miguel León-Portilla's *Time and Reality in the Thought of the Maya* (Second Edition, enlarged, University of Oklahoma: 1988):

> ... the Maya conceived of time in close association with the solar deity [kinh], something divine in itself, limitless and ubiquitous ... all the moments of time - the days, months, and years - are arrivals and presences of divine faces. They all successively come and go, letting their influences be felt, unceasingly determining life and death in the universe. Each moment is not only the presence of one god but the sum total of many presences. The deities of the numbers, those of the days, months, years, and other time measurements, come together in different points of arrival throughout the cycles. The resultant of their forces colors reality with multiple tints. Such was the universe in which the Maya lived and thought...

> ... Upon this base some preliminary conclusions and some hypotheses can be formulated at this point:
> a) The concept of time, an abstraction arrived at through experiencing the cyclic action of the sun and of the day which is its creature, was universally present among the Maya...
> b) Kinh, sun-day-time, is a primary reality, divine and limitless. Kinh embraces all cycles and all the cosmic ages. That is why it is possible to make computations about remote moments hundreds of millions of years away from the present. Also, because of this, texts such as the Popol Vuh [a late classic sacred text] speak of the "suns" of ages, past and present.
> c) The divine nature of kinh is not thought of as something abstract and shapeless. In it can be distinguished innumerable moments, each with its own face, carrying a burden which displays its attributes. Among the faces appearing in the diverse periods are those of the solar deity in all its forms and those of the gods and goddesses of rain, earth, corn, death, sacrifice, the great star, the moon and hunting. These faces constitute the most

> significant nucleus of the Maya pantheon.
> iv) The time universe of the Maya is the ever-changing stage on which are felt the aggregate of presences and actions of the various divine forces which coincide in a given period. The Maya strove, by means of their computation, to foresee the nature of these presences and the resultant of their various influences at specified moments. Since kinh is essentially cyclic, it is most important to know the past in order to understand the present and predict the future.
> v) The faces of time, mystical reality prompting the Mayan obsession, are the object of veneration. They determine and govern all activities...
>
> (pp. 49 and 54-55)

Tantalizing as it may be, Maya cyclic time is not, alone and by itself, an immediately available option for me. I can't just decide to switch cultures and religious/scientific beliefs out of the blue and live in the more personal "real-time" of the Maya cyclic universe.

However, neither is my compromise with my own Western social reality working for me. Being virtuous in the sense of moderate and compromising has not resolved my painful space/time issues. My sputtering efforts to adjust to my own society's shallow notions of what it means to live in all the available dimensions have not worked for me.

It seems that my yin accommodations will have to be balanced off, from now on, with more yang.

But a second Maya concept on these cosmic issues - that time and space might be two sides of the same nondualistic coin - has strong similarities to certain philosophical, religious and scientific alternatives within my Western culture. So before I can make strong yang decisions on how to change my life and my lawn, I need to look at this second intriguing idea from the Maya and also at a few similar options with roots closer to my cultural home.

The Flight of Things

As a bridge, I think of some very pertinent quotations I found in Paul Davies' *About Time: Einstein's Unfinished Revolution* (Touchstone paperback: 1995, p. 23):

And likewise time cannot itself exist,
But from the flight of things we get a sense of time...
                            Lucretius, *De Rerum Natura*

The moment you stop thought
   time too stops dead.
            Angelus Silesius

These Western writers - the 1st-century Roman poet-philosopher Lucretius and the 17th-century German poet-mystic Angelus Silesius (pseudonym of Johannes Scheffler, to whom Davies mistakenly refers as living in the 16th century; pardon my academic training) - also have a lot to offer me at this point in time and space. Perhaps, in their more extreme manifestations, some Western ideas can turn into their polar "opposites," leading to Eastern-like insights, and vice versa.

The Golden Extremes

The Motorcycle Way

In regard to the original problem with my lawn, I now realize that there must be a simple spatiotemporal solution to the entire matter. Is there a yang solution that deals with all the issues?

Yes, if space and time can first become united in my own mind. In his first book, the now-classic *Zen and the Art of Motorcycle Maintenance* (which I previously acknowledged), Robert M. Pirsig, in his former incarnation as "Phaedrus," says of the *Tao* that it means the same as Quality, though the latter is as indefinable as the former. Here is the standard translation of Chapter One of the *Tao Teh Ching*, followed by Pirsig/Phaedrus' substitutions:

> *Tao can be talked about, but not the Eternal Tao.*
> *Names can be named, but not the Eternal Name.*
>
> *As the origin of heaven-and-earth, it is nameless;*
> *As "the Mother" of all things, it is nameable.*
>
> *So, as ever hidden, we should look at its inner essence:*
> *As always manifest, we should look at its outer aspects.*
> *These two flow from the same source, though differently named;*
> *And both are called mysteries.*
>
> *The Mystery of mysteries is the Door of all essence.*
> (Tao, 1)

> *The quality that can be defined is not the Absolute Quality.*
> *The names that can be given it are not Absolute names.*

*It is the origin of heaven and earth.
When named it is the mother of all things.*

*Quality and its manifestations are in their nature the
  same...*
(Pirsig, p. 253)

Making some changes of my own in the traditional translation, regarding Tao:

*So, as ever hidden, we should look at time, its inner
  essence:
As always manifest, we should look at space, its outer
  aspects.*

And then adding the same meaning in Pirsig's interpretation:

*Quality and its manifestations - time and space - are in
their nature the same...*

This happens to be the conclusion of 20th-century quantum physics as well, which often refers to space and time as one relation, called spacetime or the curvature of spacetime. This scientific view is remembered as "Minkowski spacetime," after the physicist who publicly introduced the unified concept back in 1908. Classic New Age views of this unity and its philosophical/religious significance are articulated by Fritjof Capra in *The Tao of Physics* (Bantam edition: 1977) and by Gary Zukav in *The Dancing Wu Li Masters* (Bantam Books: 1979), and more recently in *The Seat of the Soul* (Simon & Schuster, 1989). These East/West perspectives are balanced by Paul Davies' Christian view in *God and the New Physics* (Simon and Schuster: 1983).

However, in recent years, some of the "mysticalizations" of contemporary Western physics and cosmology have come to be viewed by scientists and science writers as more like mystifications. Certainly quantum physics is consistent with a Taoist universe of continuous flow and motion, and there is little difference in the applicability of the relativity theory and the Taoist relativity of all things. But beyond these general worldviews one cannot get more specific in linking physics and Taoism because those specifics about our real world are changing from day to day - which, I guess, is pretty much Taoist after all!

This changing, non-dogmatic quality of reality is emphasized by John Boslough in his *Masters of Time* (J. M. Dent: 1992). His diatribe against the Big Bang theory of cosmogony, or the origins of the universe, is really an attempt to stop what the author sees as a new dogmatism, a self-satisfaction among scientific cosmologists who should be more open to new theories, no matter how weird. And indeed, some findings via the Hubble space telescope, which was repaired since it was launched (and after Boslough wrote his book), cast doubt on some aspects of the Big Bang explosion, the existence of dark matter, and other tenets of modern physics. Other evidence supports them.

Even the Pope endorses the essence of the Big Bang, for it obviously sounds a lot like the Biblical view of instantaneous creation of everything out of nothing; the void became light. But today we cannot really say when the Bang occurred or why the Hubble is coming up with data that could turn out to be inconsistent with it.

But physicists have no monopoly on Western attempts to grasp the nature of ultimate reality, especially the union of space and time. An inspired literary and philosophical intuition into our origins is Edgar Allan Poe's *Eureka*, 100 pages of perhaps unconscious insight into physicists' future theories of the creation of the universe and extreme precursors and elaborations of that theory - such as the Hindu-like "oscillating" universe, a nonlinear, cyclical cosmos of alternating periods of expansion and contraction. Poe foresees that by the year 2848 we will

> *have attained a point where only Intuition can aid us...*
>
> *Nevertheless, as an individual, I may be permitted to say that I cannot conceive Infinity, and am convinced that no human being can...*
>
> *It will now be understood that, in using the phrase, "Infinity of Space," I make no call upon the reader to entertain the impossible conception of an absolute infinity. I refer simply to the "utmost conceivable expanse" of space - a shadowy and fluctuating domain, now shrinking, now swelling, with the vacillating energies of the imagination.*
>
> *... the ruling idea... is this: - In the Original Unity of the First Thing lies the Secondary Cause of All Things, with the Germ of their Inevitable Annihilation.*
> (Edgar Allan Poe, *The Library of America*, 1984, pp. 1276, 1274, 1275, 1261; italics omitted)

As I mentioned, the Big Bang theory is still controversial, but gaining ground year by year, and this theory of the origins of everything is compatible either with the Poe-like vacillating universe, expanding then shrinking over and over, or with a steadily or even accelerating expansion, period. The Hubble Constant (named after the same astronomer who suggested that the universe is evolving) gives the rate of expansion.

I think Poe would be comfortable (if that is a word that could ever apply to Poe) with defining "intuition" as Jung does in "A Psychological Theory of Types": as "perception by way of unconscious contents and connections." In this sense, another advanced intuition into spacetime is the ancient Maya's, whose apparent concept of time itself has already been mentioned. According to León-Portilla (p. 85), perhaps for the Maya

> *... the spatial universe exists, changes, dies, and is reborn in each of the "suns" or ages as a consequence of the*

actions of the gods or countenances of time. Space is not static. It is the complement, the framework of colors, which from moment to moment sets up the stage for kinh. Upon it, as if determined by the rules of a game, or as in a drama developing in cycles, time displays its diverse countenances and masks successively. It is thus that kinh gives life, destroys and recreates without end the reality in which men move and think.

Does this mean that space and time basically constitute a homogeneous entity? Or, which is the same, were space and time, more than being merely related, a perfect identity in the core of Maya thought?...

There is another concept that may ultimately identify time with space. In the epic, *Cheyenne Autumn*, Mari Sandoz, who grew up around indigenous Americans, says that the Cheyenne

had a rich and mystical perception of all life as a continuous, all-encompassing eventual flow, and of man's complete oneness with all this diffused and eternal stream. It was a stream of many and complex dimensions, one in which man, the tree, the rock, the cloud, and all the other things were simultaneously in all the places they had ever been; and all things that had ever been in a place were always in the present there, in the being and occurring.
(Originally published in 1953; Avon: 1964, vii)

And what about the relationship between Quality and those "dual" dimensions, space and time? That Quality itself is identical to spacetime is hinted at by Pirsig, a.k.a. "Phaedrus." (Plato's original dramatic character Phaedrus appeared in the Dialogue of that name.

In Greek, "Phaedrus" means "wolf," and Pirsig felt that his former persona - an aggressive outsider - fit the name.)

Apparently a truly nondualistic "feel" for time and

space as a unified and nonlinear flow would, according to Pirsig's Phaedrus, result in Quality: I could excel naturally, for example, in "fixing" a motorcycle precisely because I would realize that it is not a separate "it" at all.

This is because the motorcycle and I are a single and coherent spatiotemporal assembly of sensory data. Through *wu wei*, I can just as easily get the engine running again by adjusting my own perceptions (sights, sounds, touches, etc.) as by turning a screw "out there." In fact, these two acts have the same meaning. As the Irish empiricist Bishop Berkeley said, "To be is to be perceived."

An even more radically accurate way to refer to this system is as "Hume's motorcycle," named after another famous Western empiricist, the Scot David Hume, who restricted human knowledge to sensory perceptions, mental ideas, and their internal relationships. For Hume I can alter the system I am in *only* by observing it: I can do it only by not-doing it.

If time and space are not divorced, the potential powers of two previously separated systems can combine into one larger unity with even greater potential. This is also true of individual people.

And so I come back, full circle (or full cycle), to *Teh* or Virtue.

Once I perceive time and space as a unity, it becomes possible, at least, for me to deal with my alienation from them, my lack of peace and comfort with the press of the passing of time and of the narrowing of the space around me. Time and space do not constitute the split personality of the macrocosmos or the microcosmos. Rather, time is just the inner or yin manifestation, space the outer or yang manifestation, of the Tao. Time and space become one another.

Without seeing this truth, my *Teh* is compromised, lost in constant struggles with illusion... just as futile as the way I try to separate the anthills in front from the eroding hill out back.

What the West has Lost

Let me now bring spacetime back down to earth, and look at the practical results of letting go of the precious dualisms of the West. Again, the best place to start is where many of those dualisms were formalized, and that is none other than our old friend Aristotle.

For Aristotle, the highest good - at least the highest human good - is happiness, with the moral virtues being tendencies or dispositions to choose the moderate midpoint relative to each of us, and the intellectual or mental virtues also necessary to the ideal life. Contemplative values are even closer to the divine, all the more so because they are not human (or humane) compromises.

Taoist potentiality or *Teh* often expresses itself on the human level as a tension between extremes, which Westerners tend to perceive as opposites or incompatible halves of an existential dualism.

But in Taoism they are the two sides of the coin of life. To water them down - to "moderate" them in order to control their consequences - is to weaken our ability to barter or exchange energy with the universe. At the midpoint we give less energy to the world than we have the potential to do; and then we wonder why it seems we get less and less in return.

Looking back, our Western culture does have its own hidden *Teh*-like tradition. We have already seen the seeds in Plato of a Taoist-type notion of Virtue as potential power. The other seeds of "virtue" - as the midpoint, as moderation - are also to be found in Plato's writings. This moral meaning was one among several taken up by Aristotle and then interpreted by medieval Christians as moralistic: moderation is good, excess is bad for people.

In our cultural history, it was the underground subcultures that kept alive the alternative interpretation of "virtue" as potentiality rather than as moral moderation. Lead and other metals, it was thought by alchemists, had the Virtue of turning into gold, just as the base nature of humans had the Virtue of becoming angelic or God-like or (in the mystical occult) perhaps unified with God.

Even "Eastern" and "Western" connote philosophical traditions along a dual axis, representing extreme positions rather than clear realities. Is American Indian thought Eastern or is it Western? We shall see later that it is neither. And is ancient Persian mysticism, say, Eastern or Western? Is it possible that a mystical poem such as the following, by the 12th-century poet Sana'i, is really both

> *If I could choose to come, I'd not have come;*
> *If I could choose to go, when would I go?*
> *The best would be if I had never come,*
> *And were not here, and did not have to go.*
>   (translated by Dick Davis in Borrowed
>   Ware, Anvil paperback)

The underground or Hermetic tradition in the "West" is oddly similar to the alchemical tradition of Taoist medicine in ancient China. Nowadays, when we think of Taoist medicine, we refer only to the "yin/yang" of acupuncture, accepted by Western scientists and physicians as very effective in its ability to block or transmute physical pain in patients. But centuries ago in China, Taoist sages were also engaged in alchemy and the transmutation of nature, including people.

Naturally enough, female and male sexuality, the yin and yang we all know best, must be part of human alchemy, too. (See *Tao: The Chinese Philosophy of Time and Change*, by Rawson and Legeza; Thames and Hudson: 1973; and *Tao Magic*, by Laszlo Legeza: Thames and Hudson, 1975.) Hormonal potential can be transmuted into higher spiritual states. Indeed, Tantric and Kundalini yoga, otherwise very different in their history and goals, both maintain this belief.

Friedrich Nietzsche, of all modern Western thinkers, speaks for the sexual interpretation of alchemical Virtue when he - taking a hint perhaps from Edmund Burke's philosophy of art, which in turn harked back to Plato's *Symposium* - recommends "sublimation" or transmutation of base or uncontrolled sexual impulses into the beauty of artistic creation.

Recent revelations about Sigmund Freud, who is ensconced in the public mind with the idea of sublimating but not repressing sex, show that his own theory may have been inspired by Nietzsche's, but he did not credit the latter for this most "modern" of discoveries.

Be that as it may, in order to find Quality - the *Tao* - in any aspect of life, the Wayfarer must focus on his or her potential power, his or her *Teh*. And the pursuit of Virtue as power may sometimes not be virtuous in Aristotle's sense of moral moderation. Our personal momentum keeps us on the seesaw of the extremes of thinking, feeling, and doing. The key is counterbalancing ourselves, and in so doing, living our lives to its full potential... while Aristotle's child remains restricted to the midpoint: stuck in the middle.

Fritjof Capra, in *The Tao of Physics* (p. 10), offers this Nietzschean interpretation of what I call "counterbalancing" oneself:

> *Recognizing the relativity of good and bad, and thus of all moral standards, the Taoist sage does not strive for the good but rather tries to maintain a dynamic balance between good and bad.*

The Wayfarer "does not strive for the good..."? For Nietzsche, that is correct if you regard "good" as dualistic and incompatible with its moral opposite, "evil." The two extremes are required for achieving and preserving personal balance and genuine harmony.

Nietzsche was also one of the very first to see the lethal consequences of allowing a value vacuum to build up between ancient Western dualistic ethics and the nondualistic ethics of the future. That deadly vacuum is moral relativism. But it is this anchorless relativism that Nietzsche predicted for our century, not the consequences of recognizing and respecting the extremes of our own feelings, and certainly not the extreme states that can check and balance each other within each of us.

It is even more lethal, in its eventual consequences, to confuse moral relativism with not being moderate. For, to Taoism, it is these very extremes that are necessary for balancing and checking each other, and without which no harmony in ourselves or therefore with other people and with nature are possible. What we value, we should value all the way.

Touch the Country

A Quest Vision

If you have ever wondered whether moderate and compromising measures to save the rainforests are really working, remember that we may all have to give up a lot to assure that these essentials of nature really flourish again, not just barely survive, as is the case with the present situation of political and economic compromise. Compromise alone will not bring the natural harmony that includes humans. The movement called "deep ecology" recognizes that extreme environmental measures may be needed to balance the previous extreme depredations of farming, mining, and burning off the rainforests, bringing both trees and humans together to the current crisis.

According to Nathaniel Altman, deep ecology

> is an outgrowth of early native beliefs that the Earth is a living body and that 'God' or the Great Spirit has endowed all of nature with innate wisdom, a wisdom that humans (as children of the Earth) share. Deep ecology holds that life is interconnected on the most fundamental levels, and that we must strive to listen to and understand the other voices of nature in order to better perceive the needs of our planetary home.
> (*Sacred Trees*, Sierra Club Books: 1994, p. 17)

The prospering of the tropical rainforests, with their remaining tribes, plants, and animal species within fragile ecologies, should be seen as a moral necessity, not as just another relativistically moderate opinion. This means that the ecological systems must be preserved, period - independent of whether, for example, medicines for humans can be discovered in some of the remaining plant species or of our need for the oxygen they produce. Moderate responses to an teetering imbalance will not succeed. We must strive to counterbalance the past.

In "touching the country," the ancient Maya believed in a First Tree of the World or *Yax-cheel-cab*. According again to Nathaniel Altman in *Sacred Trees* (pp. 26-27), this gigantic ceiba tree "grew at the exact center of the Earth and spread its branches through successive holes in the various heavenly realms."

However, this cultural insight and paradigm were not enough to ensure that the Maya would take adequate care of their immediate environment - probably the reason for their disappearance from history as a dominant civilization.

A similar paradigm was held by the Chibchas, "the original inhabitants of what is now Colombia... Among the Shipibo people of the Amazon basin, a *lapuna* tree is the central pillar holding up the multiple worlds of the cosmos." Talk about cutting through space and time! Note how these original American visions do not fit any of the usual East/West dichotomies.

A recent theory called Complexity studies natural events, from piles of sand on a beach to evolution itself, by looking at the interactions that occur at certain levels of complex behaviors. The most interesting events seem to occur at the border between order and chaos - literally the leading edge of complex phenomena.

For instance, pour out a bunch of grains of sand and at first you get random leveling, then more orderly and symmetrical stacks, then at a certain point the sand begins to avalanche down, and will continue always to randomize - no matter how much sand is added or how high the pile - when the slope is at that particular angle. The critical stage is the border between order and randomness, and what we call living organisms seem to be able to hold that line. Complexity theory goes beyond Chaos theory to study order as well. (See "Adapting to

Complexity" by Russell Ruthen, *Scientific American*, January 1993, pp. 130-140.)

The theory of Complexity, including the many fields under study at the Santa Fe Institute in New Mexico, seems to cross the categories of moderation and extremity. On the one hand, order and chaos are extremes of all kinds of behavior, living or not, and the equal tension of these "opposites" may be the most efficient and progressive stage of a complex system. On the other hand, this critical stage can be seen as *the* middle point between order and chaos. In fact, it makes sense to me - now that I think Complexly about living things - to comprehend this criticality as both the mid-point and the counterbalancing of order and chaos! And recently Complexity theory has been brought directly into the study of nature itself. One example is *Darwinism Evolving* by Depew and Weber (MIT Press). John Maynard Smith's sympathetic critique of this new direction is titled "Life at the Edge of Chaos?" (*New York Review of Books*, Vol. XLII, No. 4, pp. 28-30; March 2, 1995). Prof. Smith warns us to look for empirical data to verify Complex conclusions, which are described in mathematical terms.

Of course, the logical issue of drawing *any* social or cultural or personal conclusions from scientific and mathematical starting-points must not be ignored, if for no other reason than how it's been abused for the sake of everyone's favorite "ism" since Social Darwinism infuriated Darwin himself in the 19th century. But now there are other reasons to watch our own jumps in logic.

In an article in *The New York Review of Books* ("Sokal's Hoax," August 8, 1996), Nobel Prize Winner Steven Weinberg discusses the recent hoax by physicist Alan Sokal. The latter, a mathematical physicist, in an article in the cultural studies journal *Social Text*, summarized several abstruse theories in current science and satirically drew from them all sorts of "politically correct" conclusions... so subtly, apparently, that the journal editors missed the joke and published the piece at face value. (I say "apparently" because the title itself is not subtle: "Transgressing the Boundaries: Towards a Transformative Hermeneutics of Quantum Gravity.")

The move thus satirized has been a logical no-no to rigorous philosophers of science for at least a couple of centuries, since - once again - David Hume warned us not to proceed automatically from "is" to "ought" statements. Yet Hume also allowed and encouraged the illuminating role of *analogy* in informal reasoning.

An example of the use of analogical reasoning involving science is Katya Walter's *Tao of Chaos* (Element paperback, 1996). Here the items analogized are the codes inherent in DNA and in the symbolism of the *I Ching*. In fact, the author goes beyond this classic text for using yin-yang symbols to foretell the future when she says that "Analogy is imbedded into the very brush strokes" of the ancient Chinese language itself (p. 43).

While it is easy enough for mathematical physicists to make fun of the scientific ignorance of mere "cultural critics," it is also important to understand what is really behind all the current squabbles between these groups - metaphysics and ontology, the different assumptions about what is ultimately real, and "its" chief characteristics. If the hard scientists look at a summary of recent humanistic thinking, like John Lechte's *Fifty Contemporary Thinkers* (Routledge, 1994), they would notice that most post-World War II theorists question the assumption that there is a single, objective reality "out there." Yet Hume, the critic of sloppy, unscientific reasoning, also questioned that assumption, right up to the edge of pure solipsism, in which no claims at all can be made beyond the flow of our perceptions, whatever "flow," "our" and "perceptions" might mean.

So, at least by analogy, Complexity and Chaos theories suggest another way to think about "extremes," whether of objects out there or feelings in here. And now the balancing of my front and back lawns (out there) seems even more significant than ever. If Complexity theory is any guide, then perhaps what is required is not so much the correct description of natural balance, but rather the example - or even the vision - my own increasing harmony (in here) can offer other persons. I see now that I have a singular role to serve as one good example to others, independent of the way that is described.

Our Western culture's Aristotelian obsession with the supremacy of *homo sapiens*, with "rational" moderation in all things, and with the centrality of Earth in the universal scheme, make any other starting point look weird or insane. One of the few ways of attacking all these "official" Western assumptions *within* the culture is science fiction.

Over half a century ago, in 1943, Clifford D. Simak published a story, "Ogre," which describes another planet where trees and other plants are in control. The trees there are not only intelligent - they practice playing music in and among their branches, highly complex melodies that enchant and hypnotize the few humans who manage to land for a while and just listen. (*Analog: The Best of Science Fiction*, Galahad Books: 1994, pp. 32-65.)

Human greed causes several traders from Earth to try to kidnap several beatifically melodious trees, only to find in the nick of time that those who listen too long tend to become empathic and sympathetic with the plight of the intelligent trees. The humans dodge bullets from "rifle" trees and choking vines and make temporary peace with the plant life they are used to burning for fuel, eating for nourishment and cutting down for shelter against the weather. However, only the trees' sheer capacity for and threat of violence makes the humans back off.

But this will take us beyond the personal and environmental issues of harmony to the question of a general ethics. Natural harmony may start within ourselves but must be extended outward forever, beyond the trees and grasses on our lawns, beyond the trees and peoples of our neighborhood and the tropics, beyond East and West, and even beyond our planet.

"The Fate of Beasts"

That question is also about the "lower animals," our companions on the planet. The Judeo-Christian tradition gets generally poor marks on its attitude toward non-human life forms. Stanley Coren's *The Intelligence of Dogs* (Bantam paperback, 1995) finds more "humane" traditions in Christianity than in Judaism, but it seems to me that both groups have conveniently ignored such Biblical passages as Ecclesiastes 4:3, 18-21 (NAS):

I said to myself concerning the sons of men, "God has surely tested them in order for them to see that they are but beasts."

For the fate of the sons of men and the fate of beasts is the same. As one dies so dies the other; indeed, they all have the same breath and there is no advantage for man over beast, for all is vanity.

All go to the same place. All came from the dust and all return to the dust.

Who knows that the breath of man ascends upward and the breath of the beast descends downward to the earth?

Perhaps even more influential is the narrow vision of Descartes, the 17th-century philosopher who modernized and established mind-body and related dualisms, going further than Aristotle ever did on these matters. The Cartesian dualisms are incompatible with each other. Take Descartes' view of whether lower animals like dogs are creatures that feel pain. To him, they do not.

To admit they can and do could lead to the heretical position that dogs have souls, too. The Cartesian view of dogs, for instance, like so many of Descartes' views on sensitive subjects, protected the Church doctrine of his day and became the dominant view in European culture for centuries. Indeed, Descartes is one of the geniuses who pioneered modern dualistic rationalism, whether in theory of existence, theory of knowledge, theology, algebra or geometry.

Descartes had a dog whose name was Monsieur Grat. Theoretically, to his owner Monsieur Grat was just an automaton, a machine - pure matter, with so soul and therefore no mind inside the matter we call skin. And humans feel free to do anything they want to something lacking sentience. The sounds you hear from dogs are like the noises of a worn machine. Yet, according to Stanley Coren, the particular Cartesian dog known humorously as Monsieur Grat was

> *quite a pampered pet, to whom Descartes spoke in the same manner that we speak to our own dogs. He worried about the dog's health and referred to things that the dog liked or did not like and sometimes privately speculated on what the dog might be thinking.*
>
> (p. 65)

"Privately," for sure, since the ultimate Cartesian starting point and credo was "I think, therefore I am." All of his rationalist doctrines required the denial of life and value to non-human, non-religious entities.

When I, as a young philosophy major at the University of Maryland in College Park, first read Descartes, I could not believe that any such world-historical thinker could articulate such a cold, counterintuitive viewpoint, regardless of the relativity of our cultural differences over the centuries.

But this experience did make me think about the metaphysical and ethical place of animals. When I began to teach philosophy, I found a few writings by Peter Singer and others on animal rights and assigned them to my ethics students. They (and the college administration) thought I was crazy, an impression reinforced by my use of the works of Lewis Carroll in introductory logic! Singer's

Animal Liberation (1975, now an Avon Books paperback) is the classic ethical argument for animal rights.

More recently, and to me surprisingly, is the theological works of Andrew Linzey, especially *Animal Theology* (SCM Press, 1994; University of Illinois paperback, 1995). This looks at animal protection and rights from a Christian perspective. He claims to find a tradition that includes Albert Schweitzer and other ethical minds usually disregarded by professional theologians and academic philosophers. I would also add Harriet Beecher Stowe: "It's a matter of taking the side of the weak against the strong..." - precisely Linzey's view.

Schweitzer, that famously humble humanitarian, holds that I as a human being have the ethical duty to show all life "the same reverence as I do to my own," and that only practical action can express such a duty: intention alone will not do. "The good conscience," says Schweitzer, "is an invention of the devil" (*Civilization and Ethics*).

More recently, in *When Elephants Weep: The Emotional Lives of Animals* (Delacorte, 1995), Jeffrey Moussaieff Masson and Susan McCarthy show how our traditional assumptions - not only about conscience and good intentions, but also about emotions, feelings, behavior and language itself - are misused as excuses to mistreat and underestimate the "lower" animals. Less theoretical than Singer or Linzey, less mystical than Schweitzer, Masson and McCarthy nevertheless bring out our convenient disregard of beings who are often more "humane" to humans than we humans are to each other. Which attitude is the more profound, and which the more intelligent?

Yet it is easy for us to feel strongly about our companion animals and especially highly intelligent ones, and I myself am very attached to my ever-growing Rottweiler, Jack, named after Jack London; London knew that animals know how to survive and they don't give up life or loyalty without a fight. But what about other creatures that are not warm or fuzzy or smart or very large? These beings were among the greatest concerns of Gandhi and his philosophy of *Ahimsa* that has had so much influence on nonviolent change in many areas of life in this century.

A new "growth" in my backyard is forcing me to face this issue now. It's a weird cocoon-like web pouch that has been diligently constructed over the last few days in the heart of the "V" of the black locust tree, a sack of wriggling, squirming gypsy moths in the caterpillar stage, thousands of them, and looking like "The Blob" in the movie(s) of that name.

Do nothing, and these critters will grow up and probably destroy the very tree that has nourished them (at great cost, no doubt) into adult mothhood. And lots of other trees too. Kill the young caterpillars, and I have made a value choice between life forms. But I will do that no matter what.

So is a whole nest of little animals more valuable than a bunch of tree-plants?

As we know by now, this black locust and its relatives are crucial to any ecology that can hold the backyard hill together, so I choose, again, for it. I will take my ultra-yang insecticide and do away with this one festering nest, not because I disdain moths, but because some things are more valuable than others, and the clearer I am about which is which, the stronger my steps will be along the Tao.

Intelligent life of *every* kind (not necessarily analogues of my own mind) are the most important to protect, then the plants and other life forms that nourish the intelligent creatures, and lastly those living things that support the other two levels. (I hope this does not sound too much like Woody Allen's "Life is just a big restaurant.")

But things get more complicated when you take a wider view. I was about to say: When you keep an eye on living things with minimal pigeon-holing, so to speak. Then I realized that many moths (and butterflies) carry an "eyespot" pattern on their wings. This looks very much like the big round eye of a large mammal, higher up on the food chain, and must scare the hell out of predators about to spring on the moths. That's a pretty intelligent defense, is it not? The moth did not design it, of course, but then we humans did not design our real eyes, either.

The question is whether my own "Western" intelligence is too narrowly rational, too full of categorical distinctions, just plain too moderate and un-extreme. Intelligence, I must remember, is not the same as rationality: the latter is an overwhelming cultural construct, a web-like sheath covering the teeming types of intelligences that we barely understand.

But "Western" is a pretty vague word, as we have seen. When I want to understand the flip side of the dominant European-based philosophies of life, I turn to the works of Charles Walker. Here is his summary of the way the *occult* European tradition would regard the current issue:

> *The word ASTRAL is derived from the Latin word aster, which means "star"... The astral body is that which links living creatures to the starry world and gives them the potential for experiencing emotions. A plant (which has an etheric body) does not have an astral body; it therefore feels no emotion. On the other hand, all animals have both etheric and astral bodies, which is why all animals have emotions, such as joy and fear, love and anger. The astral body is the instrument by which creatures experience the world as "something outside", as an entity separate from self. All creatures with astral bodies have an emotional life which constantly drives them into motion (motion and emotion are words deriving from the same root)...*
> (*The Encyclopedia of the Occult*, Crescent Books, 1995: p. 55)

This is helpful, if difficult to implement. Are emotional creatures intelligent? Sentient, yes, but are they also intelligent or at least the same as intelligent beings? It is the essential worldview of non-Europeans that may have the last word on these matters.

All of the Western traditions of human rationality are indirectly addressed in Brian Swimme's foreword to *The Mayan Factor* by Jose Argüelles (Bear paperback, 1987: p. 10):

> *To say a vision of the universe is "reasonable" means that it fits into this modern world view... We don't need reasonable visions...*
>
> *... Dr. Argüelles knows that western science and western society's only hope for balance is by fully assimilating the cosmology of the primal peoples, and in particular that of the Maya. Why should the primal cosmologies be singled out? Because primal peoples begin with the same conviction: the Earth, the Sun, the galaxy, the universe - everything everywhere is alive and intelligent.*
>
> *What is required of us is humility...*

What humility is, and what rationality therefore can be, must be re-examined, and probably will have to be re-examined over and over again in any vision guiding our future, just as such re-examinations must have preceded the creation of many of the great visions of the past.

"Be the Pattern of the World"

Simple Cases

Know the masculine,
Keep to the feminine,
And be the Brook of the World.
To be the Brook of the World is
To move constantly in the path of Virtue
Without swerving from it,
And to return again to infancy.

Know the white,
Keep to the black,
And be the Pattern of the World.
To be the Pattern of the World is
To move constantly in the path of Virtue
Without erring a single step,
And to return again to the Infinite.

Know the glorious,
Keep to the lowly,
And be the Fountain of the World.
To be the Fountain of the World is
To live the abundant life of Virtue,
And to return again to Primal Simplicity.
(Tao, 28)

It is high time for me to return to the simplicity I spoke of as so refreshing about Taoism. Let me now give two examples in my own life of my child-like attempts to counterbalance myself. As potential models of behavior for other people to follow, I deem the first to be successful, the second a failure. But both were necessary chapters in my life's workbook.

The Taoist theme and method of simplicity is captured in Benjamin Hoff's two works, *The Tao of Pooh* and *The Te of Piglet* (Penguin Books, paperback edition, 1983 and 1992 respectively). ("Te" is another spelling of *Teh*.) In these cheerful books, Hoff finds all sorts of Taoist principles and sayings in the adorable Winnie-the-Pooh and other characters created by A. A. Milne in the first part of the 20th century. My own real-life lessons were not so upbeat at the time, however.

As to my successful experience of self-counter-balancing, it dealt, oddly enough, with my reading of Aristotle in school. When I was 17, I wrote a term paper for my high school's most advanced English class; I chose to read Aristotle's *Poetics* and compare the elements constituting a tragedy with some of Shakespeare's tragic characters. When I got the paper back, the teacher had written on the last page, "I have to give you an A, but I know you plagiarized this even though I can't prove it." End of comment.

Upset, I asked her why she concluded this at all; she responded (I do remember it word for word even after all these years): "Because no high-school student can understand Aristotle."

It did not help to explain to her that I had been reading Aristotle since I was 14, or that I was considering majoring in philosophy in college (I actually went on to receive a Ph.D. in philosophy around my 27th birthday). The pressure applied to me by that English instructor was clearly for me to get more moderate, to find a more normal midpoint between extremes, such as between not reading at all (illiteracy) and reading too much (bookishness or being a bookworm). But something kept me faithful to my excessive love of philosophy.

And it remained difficult to maintain a viable tension among my extremes: working later on to get a Ph.D. for example, while trying to build an ideal home life with a wife and two children.

The second case occurred earlier in the same high

school. One day the geometry teacher told us that we had to accept the postulates of Euclid as true; when I asked why that was, she said that Euclid's system required the postulates and that fortunately they were self-evident. I pointed out that the fifth postulate (the famous Parallel Postulate) was not self-evidently true to me. The teacher responded very irritably that if it's self-evident then it must be evident to me as well. I said no, sorry, but it was not. She said I was trying to embarrass her in front of her own class and, if I didn't stop asking these questions, she would eject me from the room.

When I said that I thought we were here to ask such questions, she really did throw me out, not for the day but for a whole week. I was so afraid of getting behind that, beginning the following week I never, ever again asked a question in that class. I thought Edna St. Vincent Millay might be right after all when she had said that "Euclid alone has looked on beauty bare."

Intimidation worked - my process of self-counterbalancing stalled when it came to working with numbers and symbols. A fear of them shattered me then and there. So I became more moderate. I gave up my extreme passion for logic and geometrical thinking... at least until years later, in my first year of graduate school, on the first day of my first required class in mathematical logic.

The graduate school professor, who had been a student of the great logician Kurt Gödel (more on him later), said that in order for mathematical logic to develop beyond - of course - Aristotle's syllogisms, it had to begin anew; for example, it had to drop Euclid's Parallel Postulate altogether!

Contemporary mathematical physics also depends on non-Euclidean geometries, that is, geometries in which there is not just one line in space parallel to another straight line. Non-Euclidean theories claimed that either there are no parallels or many parallels possible.

In fact, Einstein's relativity theories, nuclear power,

quantum theory and a lot of the other revolutionary paradigms of the 20th century - besides formal logic itself - all require the denial not only of the self-evidential nature of the fifth postulate but also the *absolute* truth of it. Non-Euclidean beauty is even more bare than its predecessor, like much of contemporary art as compared to earlier art forms that dominated the West.

How to De-Complexify

Even as that geometry class closed around my mind, in the real world beyond the high school geometry itself had opened the door to doubting the sacred Parallel Postulate of Euclid. (Euclid himself may have had doubts about it; otherwise, why did he not bother to use it in his proofs of the first 26 propositions of the *Elements*?)

Had I counterbalanced myself as a high-school math student, imagine the additional issues I could have raised way back then, such as why the unified concept of spacetime - the nondualistic basis for most astronomical and cosmological theories in the second half of the 20th century - also requires doubting the Parallel Postulate. Now I see that Pirsig's Quality does too, and Wayfaring as well.

A universe without the Parallel Postulate intact might have an overall concave curvature - this is a universe continually closing in on itself and, like the longitudinal "lines" of our Earth, no lines are parallel and all intersect. Another favorite non-Euclidean model is a convex curvature, so that spacetime keeps extending outward like the lines forming a saddle or the horn of a trombone. Einstein favored the former, but a number of recent scientific cosmologists favor the latter. The mathematical formulas allow for either view, but the Euclidean seems to work only here on Earth.

The point is that we have recently come to doubt space

as straight-line, time as linear - more assumptions of typical "rationality" - though the Maya and the Cheyenne and several of our other ancient neighbors in effect denied Euclid's Fifth Postulate centuries before modern mathematicians and scientists did. And we saw above that the Maya, those mathematical mystics, may even have known the polarity and relativity of space and time that unifies them into one cosmic force.

But in counterbalancing oneself or one's lawn, better late than never. At least I did offer my fellow students a strong example in that high-school English class, and eventually I got back on track with mathematics. More importantly, mathematics and the non-Euclidean track became attractive to my first-born son, who is now a young professor of physics and works every day in a realm of quantum mathematics that is well beyond my comprehension.

Again, only reaching and maintaining our own extremes of thoughts, feelings, and actions (which, as Aristotle recognized, are different in different people) can challenge the established "moderate" wisdom about such matters as what space and time might be. No doubt, even current theories of spacetime will settle into being middle-of-the-road (moderate) some day, and such compromises will have to be challenged by futuristic Wayfaring physicists and mathematicians. But to succeed, these future pioneers will first have to appear as extremists in the eyes of their peers.

Perhaps, in my interpretation of Wayfaring, Lao Tzu's book should be re-titled *The Power of the Way* rather that *The Way of Power*. Or *The Virtue of the Way*, rather than *The Way of Virtue*.

Anyone who loves old-time rock 'n' roll can recognize the *Teh* of Little Richard, the rhythm and blues pioneer whose nine hits between 1955 and 1957 still sound great. Here's what Geoffrey Himes, a *Washington Post* reporter, has to say about Little Richard's "lifelong struggle... waged with the competing pulls of riotous rock 'n' roll and reverential religion" (referring to the years of preaching and gospel-singing that interrupted Little Richard's commercial career a couple of times). "In fact," says Himes,

> *it's that struggle that makes Little Richard so fascinating. If this struggle hadn't created such a pressure in his music, then the release from that tension wouldn't have felt so liberating.*
> "Weekend," p. 6 (May 28, 1999)

What a perfect example of a performer's real Virtue, and a hint of how he maintained it.

But the Western culture deep inside of me keeps reminding me that none of us are pure potentiality. Just as it is with a great performer, in other people's eyes - and not just my own children's - I may very well be a pattern for them to copy or to oppose; I am a dynamic set of ethically relevant actions. And vice versa - others' actions can serve as a pattern of right and wrong for me. What we do in fact counts for others. I need to keep this in mind as I try to transform my lifestyle as well as my lawn by attaining greater Virtue or *Teh*.

The Useless Tree

A Trappist Door

*Once Chuang Chou [another name for Chaung Tzu]
dreamed he was a butterfly.
He was happy as a butterfly, enjoying himself and going
where he wanted. He did not know he was Chou.
Suddenly he awoke, whereupon he was startled to find he
was Chou. He didn't know whether Chou had dreamed he
was a butterfly, or if a butterfly were dreaming it was
Chou. But as Chou and the butterfly, there must be a
distinction. This is called the transformation of beings.*
(*Chuang Tzu*, Chapter Two, p. 80)

When we start looking for *ethical* patterns within the transformation of human beings, we must turn to the possibility of a Christian Way. To do this, we will consider the poetic "personal and spiritual interpretation" of Taoism by the late, great Trappist monk Thomas Merton in *The Way* of *Chuang Tzu* (Shambhala: 1965). This is the best way for me personally to involve Christianity - the central influence on my Western culture - in preserving this, our last world-try.

Ironically, the very first "reading" in the book is "The Useless Tree":

*Hui Tzu said to Chuang:
I have a big tree,
The kind they call a "stinktree."
The trunk is so distorted,
So full of knots,
No one can get a straight plank
Out of it. The branches are so crooked
You cannot cut them up*

In any way that makes sense.
There it stands beside the road.
No carpenter will even look at it.

Such is your teaching -
Big and useless.

Chuang Tzu replied:
Have you ever watched the wildcat
Crouching, watching his prey -
This way it leaps, and that way,
High and low, and at last
Lands in the trap.

But have you seen the yak?
Great as a thundercloud
He stands in his might.
Big? Sure,
He can't catch mice!

So for your big tree. No use?
Then plant it in the wasteland
In emptiness.
Walk idly around,
Rest under its shadow;
No axe or bill prepares its end.
No one will ever cut it down.

Useless? You should worry!
            (Shambhala Pocket Classics, 1992: pp. 49-50)

The poet Rilke says that his God is "like a knot with a hundred roots that drink in silence." Similarly, Christianity, like Taoism, is a tree full of knots, impossible to definitively "interpret." But in this uselessness lies its usefulness: Christianity (at least the original tree with its roots in the life of one carpenter who did look at it - Jesus) acts through *wu wei* - by not-doing certain things.

In his introductory remarks to the thought of *Chuang Tzu*, Merton observes that the philosopher, "surrounded by ambitious and supposedly 'practical men,' reflected that these 'operators' knew the value of the 'useful,' but not the greater value of the 'useless'" (p. 27).

Most people seem to regard Christian *humility* as "useless" in a world of obvious Darwinian competition - although a few critics, following Nietzsche, consider humility as downright dangerous and hypocritical. Humility is exemplary of true Christianity because it is so characteristic of Jesus himself and much less so of the Christian churches founded in his name.

Helping to keep humility alive as a primary stance toward nature is the Theology of Humility advocated by John Templeton, including his foundation's Humble Approach Initiative. That program seeks "to bring about the discovery of new spiritual information by furthering high-quality scientific research," which sounds paradoxical but fits tongue-and-groove with Wayfaring.

It is interesting to recall that my favorite expression, the Way, was sometimes used in the Bible to refer to the humble path of Jesus himself. I began thinking about these things some years ago, in California, when I was recovering from a long illness. As soon as I had the energy to hike a little again, I walked every day to what people call "The Monastery" in Sierra Madre, actually the Mater Dolorosa Passionist Retreat Center, where I would first warm up by walking the Stations of the Cross. (Since that time the Stations and the Garden have been renovated and updated, with the help of good fundraising.) Then, avoiding the rattlesnakes behind the Center, I would cross over into the dry hills of the San Gabriel Mountains, each day walking just a few more yards.

The Monastery was so peaceful that it might have been the last place in the south-facing San Gabriels where the rattlers felt safe! What is the sound of one snake rattling? A sound that makes you very humble. And that can mean life or death when you are up in those hills all by yourself.

Which I did over 100 times in the '80s. In many of those solitary expeditions I crossed paths with an elderly man whom I called Methuselah, and in turn he would call me Moses, because I always carried a walking stick taller than I was.

I eventually learned that Catholic Passionists try to blend the worldly ways of the Jesuits with the solitariness favored by Trappists like Thomas Merton. And according to Merton, competing values at the heart of Christianity, such as love of neighbor or compassion and duty, are not as characteristic of Christianity as humility is. In fact, he says, they are also part of the classic philosophy of Confucius, who was himself considered a competitor of Chuang Tzu. But the "Aristotelian" side of Confucius (Kung Fu-Tse) made him emphasize the social rules according to which such values must be expressed, whereas Jesus of Nazareth and Chuang Tzu definitely did not. Merton says that humility

> manifests itself everywhere by a Franciscan simplicity and connaturality with all living creatures. Half the "characters" who are brought before us to speak the mind of Chuang Tzu are animals - birds, fishes, frogs, and so on. Chuang Tzu's Taoism is nostalgic for the primordial climate of paradise in which there was no differentiation, in which man was utterly simple, unaware of himself, living at peace with himself, with Tao, and with all other creatures. But for Chuang this paradise is not something that has been irrevocably lost by sin and cannot be regained except by redemption. It is still ours, but we do not know it, since the effect of life in society is to complicate and confuse our existence, making us forget who we really are by causing us to become obsessed with what we are not...
>
> (pp. 32-33)

Perhaps we would remain humble if we were not continually tricked by the social game into actually believing what others may (at least for a while) think about us. In social existence, to be humble would be to accept ourselves as we are; and what would the economy be like if we all did that? Ambition, wealth, career ladders, and other embodiments of yang control would themselves be useless then, rather than serving as the very definition of usefulness, as is the case in nearly all modern social structures. And speaking of structures...

The Tree of Life, like the World Tree of the rainforest peoples, is a metaphor used by many other cultures, from Judeo-Christian (the Tree of Life in Genesis was the "other" tree that could have been chosen instead of the Tree of Knowledge) to Amerindian (such as the pine tree Deganawidah planted - the "genesis" of the Iroquois), and from early Hinduism to ancient Scandinavian mythology.

The Tree of Life is a "useless" tree if worldly power is our life's goal - the Tree of Knowledge is more appropriate to that. Merton's Jesus indicates that each of us, sooner or later, will have to choose between these cosmic trees. My black locust tree reminds me of this ethical dilemma.

So does an article in the Religion section of the *Washington Post* (June 26, 1999, p. B9), about Vigen Guroian, a lay member of the Armenian Orthodox Church, for whom

> *gardening is a form of meditation, but one that is more active than passive. The role of a gardener is "not just seeing, but doing and smelling..."* ... *He also decided to include biblical plants such as lilies, hyssop, leeks, mint, mustard and juniper...*

That seems to be one way to choose the path of Merton's Jesus. I say "*Merton*'s Jesus" to indicate that I trust that monk's grasp of the "original face" of Christianity. Less-monastic, more popular interpretations of the teachings of Jesus tend to put less emphasis on his humility and more on his "powers." Check out *Who's Who in the Bible* (p. 215), where, under the heading "The Master of Nature," the editors of the popular *Reader's Digest* state regarding the life of Jesus:

> ... When a seasonal storm struck his boat on the Sea of Galilee, he stilled the wind and waves in a dramatic demonstration of his mastery of nature. Such nature miracles were not uncommon in Hebrew Scripture, of course, and ranged from Moses' parting the Red Sea to Joshua's calling for the sun to stand still at Gibeon.

Whether people saw these non-natural events as miracles or as tremendous powers, they had the effect of boosting religious belief, Jewish and Christian. (Moses, with his Egyptian name and upbringing, might well have known how to take advantage of the interval between low and high tide in what was probably a body of water much smaller than the Red Sea.) There is little in the way of humility in any of these unmonastic interpretations.

There is an astonishing book by Zane Grey called *The Vanishing American* - at least the original version published as a serial in 1922, before its anti-missionary story of the love between an American Indian man and a white woman was expurgated in book form - in which the humble Nophaie tries to synthesize Christianity and Indian religion. It is no accident that Grey composed for his original story some of the most intense, impressionistic descriptions of the beauty and harshness of nature I've ever read. If the (original) Christian Way is viewed as Merton's Way of humility, and if humility - as Chuang Tzu and Thomas Merton and Zane Grey's Nophaie understand it - is behaving socially in ways consistent with our genuine *pre-social* self, how can such a "natural" person ever survive in a tough yang economy? Recall as well the quotation above on how humility is needed to grasp other visions like the ancient Maya's. But in modern times *money* is the spatial medium of the nonmaterial social mores in which we must swim like a fish or sink like a stone.

Direct Intuition

So the real question is my own survival! Humility, essential as it is in the Mertonian sense, will not be sufficient for my survival inside economic walls. *Intuitive* knowledge, plus some other Virtues to be mentioned, will also be crucial for me:

Chuang Tzu and Hui Tzu
Were crossing the Hao river
By the dam.

Chuang Tzu said:
"See how free
The fishes leap and dart:
That is their happiness."

Hui replied:
"Since you are not a fish
How do you know
What makes fishes happy?"

Chuang said:
"Since you are not I
How can you possibly know
That I do not know
What makes fishes happy?"

Hui argued:
"If I, not being you,
Cannot know what you know
It follows that you
Not being a fish
Cannot know what they know."

Chuang said:
"Wait a minute!
Let us get back
To the original question.
What you asked me was

> 'How do you know
> What makes fishes happy?'
> From the terms of your question
> You evidently know I know
> What makes fishes happy.
> I know the joy of fishes
> In the river
> Through my own joy, as I go walking
> Along the same river."
> (Merton, pp. 143-144)

This story is a reminder of the pivotal role of intuition in decisions. Robert Browning says that:

> *Truth is within ourselves, it takes no rise*
> *From outward things, whate'er you may believe*
> ... *and to* know
> *Rather consists in opening out a way*
> *Whence the imprisoned splendour may escape,*
> *Than in effecting entry for a light*
> *Supposed to be without.*

Robert Browning the Western poet, Chuang Tzu the Eastern philosopher, Thomas Merton the Christian ascetic - even Plato, who always turned eventually to fables and extended metaphors - all recognize when the usefulness of logic ran out, and that is when they turn to intuition. As I decide my own future I need to balance rigorous analytic logic (yang) with my yin intuitions about who I really am behind and beyond the social/economic veneer. I need not focus on what I am not. In intuitive moments or even seconds I can observe the humble self - "the imprisoned splendour" - trying to open out a way, or Way.

While I attempt to counterbalance rigorous analysis with intuitive realization, I think of Merton, who goes even farther when it comes to the place of intuition in decisions:

The wise man therefore, instead of trying to prove this or that point by logical disputation, sees all things in the light of direct intuition. He is not imprisoned by the limitations of the "I," for the viewpoint of direct intuition is that of both "I" and "Not-I." Hence he sees that on both sides of every argument there is both right and wrong. He also sees that in the end they are reducible to the same thing, once they are related to the pivot of Tao.

When the wise man grasps this pivot, he is in the center of the circle, and there he stands while "Yes" and "No" pursue each other around the circumference.

The pivot of Tao passes through the center where all affirmations and denials converge. He who grasps the pivot is at the still-point from which all movements and oppositions can be seen in their right relationship. Hence he sees the limitless possibilities of both "Yes" and "No." Abandoning all thought of imposing a limit or taking sides, he rests in direct intuition...
(Merton, pp. 60-61)

Can I pivot in the stillpoint (recall the "Centre" of Ssu-Kung Tu) between the "Yes" and "No" of life-changing issues, and can I do this if I cannot even resolve my lawn problems? Is not the pivot of problems also the heart of those problems? What else, beyond Merton's "direct intuition," must a humble Wayfarer do in order to be pivotal to the Tao?

Thomas Merton might have turned at this point to Willa Cather's tough statement: "I like trees because they seem more resigned to the way they have to live than other things do."

But I am no monk, so before going deeper into the concept of intuition, I want to be clear in my own mind about what I need to do - even if that appears completely useless to others - if I am to assist the last world.

A Mental Fear of Space

The Wisdom of Nature

Something more *is* needed besides Thomas Merton's "humility" and "direct intuition" if we are to succeed in implementing Taoist-like principles in the modern urban world. Later we will look more closely at intuition. But first, I mentioned that Christianity does not have a monopoly on certain "values" it is best known for, such as compassion; whereas humility, as Merton emphasizes, is a value it shares with few Ways other than Taoism. For both Ways, the humble person is the natural person, the one who can face God or other people without his or her social mask interfering:

The Lord of All to us is all unknown.
And yet these Woods and Springs must
Some One own.
Let us not murmur if our Wine we Buy:
In our own Purse have we Sufficiency.

This Transcendentalist poem is not from Thoreau or Emerson, or even Robert Frost, but from the Taoist poet Ho Chih-Chang. Clearly, as contrasted with Christianity, Taoism focuses much more on humility than on compassion, although we will see that this point depends on what we and the ancient Taoists mean by the latter word. This preference for humility is due to the Taoist value of naturalness, of being part of and not separate from the natural environment.

To turn us back to Natural purity
Is, after all, the highest State.
       (Both poems above in Van Over, pp. 244-245)

We do find intimations of this view in a minority of Christians. I discovered this inadvertently one day when I was hiking alone, on a very misty early morning, in the San Bernadino Mountains of Southern California. Both the San Bernadinos and their neighbors to the west, my dusty San Gabriels, feel like giant piles of gravel under your feet. This particular morning a shale shift or small earthquake revealed a hole in the ground, and down there at the bottom lay a book.

It was in fine condition, having obviously been buried there for many, many years. I still have that book, entitled *The Simple Life*, by Charles Wagner (Grosset & Dunlap, 1901). I wondered if perhaps a community of Transcendentalists or Arts and Crafts pioneers had an experimental community up here, far away from the urban sprawl to come. On the last page Wagner writes:

> *The spirit of simplicity is a great magician. It softens asperities, bridges chasms, draws together hands and hearts... This is the true social cement, that goes into the building of a people.*

I suppose to some developers these mountains must look like potential goldmines of gravel for real cement and big buildings. Back in my home in Sierra Madre, I thought: How ironic - gravel is the modern treasure hidden within the San Bernadino and San Gabriel Mountains. I can see the headlines now: "Gravel discovered in California!!!!"

I recently looked up what this first edition of the wisdom of simplicity might be selling for on Internet auction sites: up to $15! Clearly, in comparison to a Wagner or a Merton, most Christians and other contemporaries put natural simplicity at a lower priority than compassion, and plants and animals well below humans. But over the centuries this has resulted in emphasizing compassion for other humans rather than for any and all living things. God is above nature to most Westerners; within nature to most Taoists.

It is no coincidence that the "secret" Taoist classic, the *Wen Tzu* - the very name does not appear in the title of the Cleary translation of "the long-forgotten sequel to the *Tao Te Ching*" - dwells extensively on what it means for humans to be part of nature. No wonder this book is almost unknown to Westerners:

> *In the vast unknown, rely on the power of Nature, sharing the same energy as Nature.*
> (*Wen Tzu*, #149)

Nevertheless, most of us must live with and within an economy as well, and rely on its power, natural or not. Plants and fellow animals do not have to worry about financial survival, though they clearly do have to worry about real cement.

And there is no doubt that complex economies, among other changes since the time of Jesus and the original Taoists, have made it more difficult for working people to be both "natural" and economically successful. The results are not only alienation from one another and stress levels that kill - they also include our ever-increasing alienation from our natural environment. This deadly trend appears to be more economic than religious in its genesis.

But while economic thinkers in the 19th century, such as Marx and Engels (who were powerfully influenced by the Romantic image of the pre-industrial American Indian), concluded that such alienation from nature would occur through sheer exploitation of the working class, what eventually occurred is almost the opposite... the exploitation, overworking and overuse of natural "resources" gradually engulfed much of the human population as well. And now nature is rebelling against workers as well as property owners, including those of us who are both.

To be fair, if Merton were alive today, he would probably remind us that, long before modern environmentalism, even before what Joseph Campbell calls "monomyths" - such as the *Star Wars* films - Genesis had warned us of what greed does to any Garden of Eden, East or West.

What can we do realistically to re-unite with nature? For that is what is needed on top of following Merton's and our own direct intuition. What can *I* do, either with my lawn or my economic roles, to heal the unnatural and anti-nature rift between people and their natural environment? To help them grab their last chance, their last world?

First, we have to preserve, while we can, the "nature wisdom" of native peoples. Works such as *Wisdom of the Elders* (Suzuki and Knudtson, Bantam: 1992) and *Wisdom Keepers* (Wall and Arden, Beyond Words: 1990) have made a good start on this endeavor by capturing both the poetry and the science of ancient indigenous people. Nathaniel Altman's *Sacred Trees* covers the tree-wisdom of native peoples around the world. Later we will look more closely at our own Native American Way. The nature wisdom of such native cultures as the Mapuche (referring to "people of the Earth") of southern Chile deserves to be saved as much as nature itself.

Empathy Helps

Also helpful in healing the growing dualism between us and nature is what I call "empathy." The word "empathy" is a modern word that captures, in my opinion, some very old, very valuable ideas, some of them apparently central to the teachings of Jesus and a number of his followers like St. Francis of Assisi, as well as some more recent and surprising thinkers, some Christian, some not Christian, and some a bit of both.

To be even more specific, because it is important to differentiate between empathy and the related modern concepts of compassion and sympathy, the term "empathy" was coined by the American psychologist Edward Titchener. He devised the word as a translation of the German expression *Einfuhlung*, which literally means "feeling into."

The idea of Einfuhlung came from several 19th-century philosophers of art, who in turn traced their thoughts back to Immanuel Kant and to another old friend, David Hume, inventor of the *wu wei* "motorcycle."

Kant upholds the Golden Rule - Do unto others as you would have them do unto you - by giving it a rational and updated foundation, his Categorical Imperative: to do the morally right thing, always intend to treat other people as ends in themselves, and never solely as a means to your own ends or ambitions. But since we cannot control other people's behavior or the consequences of their "intentions" or our own, it must be those intentions themselves upon which moral judgments depend. Kant thinks of these intentions more as the goals or purposes of actions than as their psychological causes or stimuli.

So it is the rationality (noncontradictory nature) of these internal "maxims" that constitutes the foundation of the "metaphysics of morals." The term maxim was also used by Aristotle to refer to a syllogism's major premise, the basic assumption of a formal logical argument, at least before the advent of post-Aristotelian symbolic logic. But though a maxim as purpose can become rational, and must be to be called moral, its birth or genesis is really in our feelings, and in our ability to intuit or feel the similar feelings and emotions of others.

Hume, in turning against Kant's faith in rationalizing our feelings and emotions, concludes that "Reason is, and ought only to be the slave of the passions" (*Treatise o̧ Human Nature, 1739-40*, Book II, Part III, Section III). For Hume, as with the Masters of Huainanzi, reasoning is limited to factual and logical relationships, and ethics is neither. For the latter, nonrational, emotive factors are and must always be central.

To make a Humean ethical judgment, we must rely on

"sympathy," specifically how we believe a hypothetical but sympathetic observer *would* feel about the observed person or action. A similar theory - "the man within the breast" - was articulated by Hume's friend, Adam Smith, in 1759. Nineteenth-century "empathy," as a blend of Kantianism and Hume's early utilitarianism, can be seen as the counterbalancing of Kant's extreme rationalism (absolute rules determined by categories of rational thought and logic) and Hume's extreme emotivism, where there is no relationship between logic and our conclusions about right and wrong, good and evil. Even before Hume and before Kant, there are traces of empathy as we know it today in the ethical philosophies of the Moral Sense school earlier in the 18th century and of the 17th-century philosopher, Baruch Spinoza. We will say more about Spinoza shortly.

Since Hume's use of "sympathy" predates the invention of "empathy," we need to see that the former is closer to the latter than to our contemporary use of "sympathy." The latter, like "compassion," means feeling-along-with: parallel feelings between distinct people. Empathy means feeling-inside: people feeling the same thing, sharing the same experience, at one and the same time.

Metaphorically, empathy is synchronous and non-Euclidean, while sympathy is linear and Euclidean, where one experience parallels - and thus is never identical to - another. Sympathy or compassion, as we understand them today, such as feeling sorry for someone in their misfortune, keeps people separate, while empathy unites them in the same emotional experience.

It is not for me to say how empathy works, but it does, if we let it. Psychological research on the topic stretches from the bibliographies given in *Empathy I* and *Empathy II* (edited by Lichtenberg, Bornstein and Silver; Erlbaum, 1984) to Carol Gilligan's *In a Different Voice* (Harvard, 1982) and follow-up work by her and others since. But for me the most significant scientific work on empathy is found in the monographs of Heinz Kohut.

According to Kohut's "self psychology," lack of empathy characterizes the narcissistic personality disorders. Successful psychoanalysis "will increase... empathic ability," he states in *The Analysis of the Self* (International Universities Press, 1971). Empathy, says Kohut, is "a mode of observation," and not itself an explanation of disorders.

A mode of observation or perception is exactly what Hume thinks empathy (his "sympathy") is: for him, that is all it could be! Yet, perhaps empathy is really more than that, possibly a separate sense, a kinesthetic-like perception that is possible between two or more persons - and also between people and the other sentient beings of nature.

Hume himself limits us to our five senses and the ideas formed out of them and their interactions, but some later thinkers consider a "moral sense" to be at work as well, at least among most human beings. However, the experience of empathy is as simple as allowing ourselves to feel the pain of our injured dog, the terror of wild elephants on the run, or the grief of a widowed neighbor.

Believe it or not, it was an art historian who first suggested how to apply empathy to life, even though he himself restricted his view to experiencing artistic beauty. The lessons from his research are still valuable today in that they teach us about the general nature of nondualistic social experience... how people, in their efforts to be whole and full of integrity, can join with other people and even other beings on the emotional level of shared experience. Such experience, it will be found, is necessary to make sound moral judgments - conclusions about what is right and wrong based on adequate information, including perceptions of the emotional state of other living things who are involved in the current situation or affected by it.

The art historian was Wilhelm Worringer, who wrote *Abstraction and Empathy* in 1908. He appeals to the concept of empathy in order to help explain what beauty is and why the form of or in an object of art appeals to us. For him, empathy is a means of fusing or uniting a subject (observer) and object (work of art) as "the inmost connection between the I and the work of art."

In this light, the concept of empathy can be extended beyond Worringer's aesthetics and regarded as a means of transcending in general the traditional dualism between subject and object, observer and observed, perceiver and perceived, knower and known. An overcoming of such separateness is the root of mystical experience, of Pirsig's quest for Quality, of the Maya spacetime unification, of the Amerindian vision quest, like the sundance or fasting in the wilderness, and of Zen meditation.

And not just Zen meditation: according to Melville in Moby Dick, "Meditation and water are wedded for ever," a sentiment any whale-lover or any Taoist would share.

Abstraction

To comprehend how empathy can play such a profound role in ethical experience, even in what goes on in our own front or backyard, let us first understand its role in the experience of art according to Worringer. And to do this we need to contrast, as he does, empathy with abstraction. Empathy and abstraction are the two modes of appreciating art, says Worringer.

Some works of art - almost any of Van Gogh's come to my mind, but in particular "The Potato Eaters" or "Wheatfield with Crows" - elicit our emotions and in addition (for even Nazi propaganda films did that) we identify with the emotions portrayed, represented, or expressed. In terms of the emotions, the observer of art is no longer distinct from the painting.

That is one way in which art helps to temporarily get rid of the self, the overarching ego that otherwise stands between the appreciator and the appreciated. The other way, says Worringer, is abstraction. Here, we do not engage our real feelings as we do in empathic experience - in abstraction our feelings are withheld from the art object. When we abstract, it might be said, we subtract our emotions from the aesthetic experience.

Instead, when we are in the abstract mode we contemplate only the geometry and formal qualities of the piece. These qualities represent permanence and stability; empathy certainly does not. Neoclassical art is best appreciated in the abstract mode, and so are the geometrical paintings of Rothko, and the formal lines of Brice Marden, whom John Richardson calls "arguably the finest abstract painter of his generation." The ultimate art of abstraction would seem to lie in mathematical or other pure forms.

And no doubt Worringer himself missed out on some later artists who, like Jackson Pollock or M.C. Escher, might best be appreciated through a balance of *both* modes. Either mode - empathic or abstract - can bring about that temporary loss of the sense of self that permits us to meld with art: emotional fusing through empathy, intellectual fusing through abstraction... feelings and forms.

However, Worringer has a warning for those who abstract a lot and who cannot seem to empathize through art: practicing abstraction alone is "the result of a great inner conflict between man and his surroundings... " and of "a mental fear of space."

The Zophar Effect

What does all this say about my lawn and me? Should I myself heed Worringer's warning? Is it possible that I, in my Angst-ridden decision process concerning lawn and lifework, have been too abstract and not empathic enough to be able to make the right decisions in the art of living?

It is I, not Worringer, who applies his philosophy of art to ethics. Highly empathic people, I maintain, can leap the existential gap and feel exactly what others feel while they are feeling it. Ethically speaking, this is precisely what allows us in the first place to "Do unto others." Empathy puts us in their emotional shoes, at least for a while.

True enough, brilliant abstracting can also figure out, logically, what others would do unto me, as based on a study of their observable and quantifiable forms (patterns) of behavior. But ethical abstraction by itself just increases the emotional gap, the communication space between individuals. As David Hume and the Masters of Huainan might have said, behavioral forms by themselves cannot lead to knowledge of right and wrong, or of what is good and bad.

In the biblical story of Job, one of his three friends, Zophar, condemns him and shows no empathy at all for the long-suffering Job, who has lost his ten children, his health, and his livestock. This lack of empathy, joined with a moralistic and judgmental attitude toward the suffering of others, I call the Zophar Effect. Zophar is always the last of Job's friends to speak, symbolic of the weak ethical stature of anyone who exchanges empathy for abstract judgment.

So it should be clear that I am not denying that there is a right and a wrong - I am just affirming a non-abstract Way to arrive at such an ethical conclusion. And, as will be seen in the next chapter, I also affirm "third" values that sometimes go beyond this dualism, and so must stand on its shoulders to see farther ahead.

As Chuang Tzu almost says (in Merton's rendition

previously quoted) when the Taoist reacts to the logical abstractions of Hui Tzu: nature is full of feeling things, what Buddhists call sentient beings, and so we are capable of feeling both the grief of the widow and the joy of the gliding fish... at the very same time they are experiencing these feelings.

But finally, another "old one" ("tzu"), another Western "father" - Aristotle again - would caution me here against having too much empathy as well as too little. The black locust tree in my back yard is not more important to "feel into" than is my frustrated neighbor. Nor is the experience of empathy the same as feeling sorry for anyone, especially not for myself, for having to earn a living in this world.

The last remaining coal miners across the state line in West Virginia have little time for empathizing with me in my minor plight while they inhale coal dust. As a child here in Maryland I used to hear their "hillbilly" songs over the radio, but I was too young to understand that many were about coal-mining life in West Virginia. Come to think of it, these mountaineers usually sang about loss of jobs, their health, and loved ones. Blue Grass musicians still do, even with the old coal mines closed down.

Nowadays the big energy companies find it cheaper to just decapitate the mountaintops of West Virginia to reach the remaining coal, haul it out with gigantic machines, dump the rest in the streams, then abandon the site and move on to the next mountaintop. A Shakespeare sonnet says it perversely well, so well that it makes me want to keep returning to West Virginia:

> *Full many a glorious morning have I seen*
> *Flatter the mountain-tops with sovereign eye,*
> *Kissing with golden face the meadows green,*
> *Gilding pale streams with heavenly alchemy.*

Empathy for living things is important in rounding out Lao Tzu's and Chuang Tzu's Taoism - supplementing its "direct intuition" - for modern Wayfarers, and Western tradition is crucial for adding that. Empathy, along with nature wisdom and Mertonian humility, helps heal the dualistic rift not just between people and nature - like between the ants and me in the front yard - but also between us and other humans. Francis of Assisi sees all of these connections when he says:

> *If you have men who will exclude any of God's creatures from the shelter of compassion and pity, you will have men who will deal likewise with their fellow men.*

Why not take this sentiment to its extreme? Beyond people, even beyond ants. What about the grass that makes up my lawn, or at least the non-ant parts of it? In his poem "Grass," Carl Sandburg speaks for that inarticulate part of nature:

> *I am the grass.*
> *Let me work.*
>
> *I am the grass; I cover all.*

The Third Side of Life

Beyond Empathy

Nothing I said in the previous chapter should be construed as disparaging logic in its own realm - the interaction of ideas in the human mind. In fact, there is a logical connection between Worringer's aesthetic and the ethics of empathy - I mean a conceptual relationship, not just the historical fact that I borrowed his theory of aesthetics, though I do believe that theory helps formulate an ethical supplement to augment Asian and Native American views. And a boat cruise described two chapters on will illustrate the need for logic to balance off empathy and intuition.

And sometimes in life, empathy does not work. Even if we believe in a sixth sense, a kind of interpersonal kinesthesia - and I have made it clear that my experience does lead me to that belief - this does not mean it's always operative or accurate. Another person may be giving misleading information or she may be confused by repression or illness.

In such cases I apply "analogy" - I note the physical behaviors and conclude, by analogy to my own actions in similar cases, that the other person is probably (though not certainly) motivated by the same kind of emotions that I feel or would feel in such contexts. This is abstraction coming to the rescue of empathy. It is an experience that is both, and perhaps in equal measure, what Worringer would call abstract thinking and empathic feeling.

For now, creative people like Worringer's artist or Edgar Allan Poe have a real advantage over the rest of us. When analogy is utilized, even though analytic logic helps us generalize to new cases, it is the *imagination* that extends and expands our emotions. In experiencing empathic analogues - for instance when I see a car accident, and I feel the pain of the trapped victim, even though I've never lived through such a horror - neither reflection nor recollection is enough to enable us to share the full experience.

So an imagination that is highly developed can more quickly reconstruct what such a violent experience *would* feel like. It seems to follow that, as ethical relationships frequently depend on empathy, and empathy often on imagination, the more imaginative we are or can become, the more sound (more grounded in social reality) our ethical judgments will be... what is right and wrong to do, good and bad to value or judge. The moral imagination is often the way to moral reality.

I remember way back now, years ago in graduate school, the pull of that great, little-known (at least to the public) American philosopher C. S. Peirce, the first real pragmatist, and especially his insight into utilizing non-factual phrases like "would feel" to step beyond the here-and-now. What Peirce would have us enter is the world of real generalities, laws that exist independently of our own experiences.

Ultimately and ideally, I see now that we should be capable of having so much empathy that, à la Worringer, we could temporarily experience loss of the strong sense of self, of ego, and could (at least briefly) be united emotionally with the other person or being.

With enough imagination and linguistic flexibility, we should be able to empathize with more and more creatures all the way to the point where we have empathy with all living things, as Gautama Buddha and Jesus Christ appeared to have.

But to take a case literally close to me, if I am to personally join in such unity with other beings, something that might be called "the analogical imagination" needs to be part of my life, especially of my ethical decisions about my lawn and my future livelihood. Perhaps it is fitting that it takes the imagination to cope with the large issues of how I relate to time and space. I may need to apply Worringer's aesthetics in order to practice using my own imagination, first in empathizing more and more with greater numbers of people, then empathizing with other types of sentient beings and ultimately - I guess this is usually considered the mystical leap - with all of nature.

Whose Intuition?

Empathy and intuition are aspects of another side of life. We have seen Thomas Merton using "direct intuition" to explain Taoism, particularly how it avoids the dualism or digitizing of true and false, right and wrong. Intuition is able to break free from the useful but limited base of twoness, which, like computers, is rational and digital, while intuition is non-rational and many-valued.

The latter is what the Swedish poet Gunnar Ekelöf calls "the third side of life." Between Yes and No is Maybe, or perhaps the Japanese "Mu." Beyond True and False there is Neither, or the Zen *koan*. In addition to Right and Wrong is Nietzsche's Immoral, which today would be better phrased as the Nonmoral. Ekelöf the poet, the word-artist, speaks of

Those who have never forgotten that gray is gray...
only taking with them what is undecided and
undecidable.

There, on the third side of life,
where it is neither black nor gray nor white,
and out of the three is created an immense number
beyond all values, truths and lies.
    (Ekelöf, "Variations" in *Friends, You Drank Some*
    Darkness, trans. by Robert Bly; Beacon, 1975: p. 93)

Living the third side of life is perceiving the "third value" in any dualistic series, including but not limited to empathic and intuitive experience.

Intuition takes over cosmology when rational thought is insufficient for comprehending spacetime and its local manifestations.

For instance, in the middle of an argument, I suddenly realize that the solution lies neither in my opponent's view nor in my own. Some third possibility - neither of the two opposing opinions, or perhaps both of our views simultaneously - is the intuitive response that comes to me. The same intuitive thinking can occur in politics or religion...

... or in physics or biology or mathematics. Mathematical logicians refer to a system with three "truth values" as intuitionist: imagine a computer whose logic is made up of 1's, 0's and 1/2's. That would put digital microchips out of business! - and create a whole new business for intuitionist logicians to build and program futuristic computers, probably biologically based. I would suggest calling the latter "Base B" to show how different in principle their theorems or true conclusions will be from those of the non-biological number systems like Base 2 or Base 10.

To go even further, we must go back in time, to 1931, when the great logician Kurt Gödel - the mentor of my professor in that first graduate class in mathematical logic - proved logically that some truths can never be *proven* true. In a sense, this is logical proof that logic cannot prove everything, that the very essence and possibility of rational thinking requires third values... intuitive conclusions not subject to logical proof. As we will see later on, the consistency of higher mathematics logically requires logic to be limited in power.

Metaphorically, an intuition is a "holographic" experience. It is like viewing a whole forest, all at once and three-dimensionally, rather than seeing it tree by tree while walking through it step after step. People who count on their intuitions use them as short cuts across spacetime. This is true of scientists as well as religious mystics, fundraisers as well as Taoists.

In physics, for instance, picture the atom with an encircling electron at both one level or valence and a different valence at the same time - physicists have to try to imagine this all the time, because quantum mathematics requires it to be the case. Perhaps this is why Albert Einstein, sounding like Edgar Allan Poe in *Eureka*, claims that "The really valuable thing is intuition." Wayfarers of all types would certainly concur on the essential role of intuition in stepping outside of ordinary either/or perceptions and judgments to gain the whole picture - not to deny those perceptions and judgments so much as to ensure their integrity.

Biology Too

Last and certainly not least, consider biology itself. Creatures have been discovered that are neither organic nor inorganic. Is the whole cosmos alive or not? Over two hundred years ago, our "motorcycle" friend, David Hume, logically demonstrated that the existence of such an organism - or indeed of any universal "design" at all, living or not - cannot be logically demonstrated.

Perhaps we can only know the cosmic design, at least as far as life is concerned, through philosophic or religious intuition. Plato certainly thinks so.

And, as Marjorie Spiegel (no relation) asks in *The Dreaded Comparison: Human and Animal Slavery* (Mirror Books, 1996), must every biological thing always be divided dualistically, the human from the nonhuman, the human from "animals," the mammals from other animals? The Maya of our own continent seem to have made no such distinctions. Is it just a coincidence that they had a very different system of numbers for counting, computing, keeping their historical records, and predicting events a million years into the future?

True, humans can conceptualize or think - here we recall Aristotle's definition of a human being as the "rational animal." And rationality is wondrous (just go ahead and ask its opinion on that). But when intuition is included, "thinking" is much wider than just "reasoning." People can think without necessarily reasoning, without linear, stepwise logic - so why can't certain other animals think by intuiting but not by reasoning?

If, like so many of this century's philosophers of science and linguistic philosophers, we appoint *language* as the essence of both human-ness and rationality, then most other animals (which ones is debatable) are not rational and cannot think; but then, what about our cavemen and cavewomen ancestors, who for a long period apparently had no language either? Were they not human? Could they not think? Perhaps it would have been better if some Martians had landed a few hundred thousand years ago and, with the kindest of intentions, put collars around the necks of our oldest relatives and kept them as pets. (Result: a Planet of the Apes?)

And though we humans revel in our unique rational abilities, what nonrational, intuitive, thinking (as well as empathic feeling) processes are we ignoring in our all-out quest for economic subsistence and control over nature? What can we learn from "lower" beings about how to live our lives? Only our ancient Western divorce from nature could make this sound like a silly question. Even (or especially) Darwin, the founder of evolutionary theory, considered it a very serious question. That point is sadly forgotten in academic biology or evolution classes.

The primate psychologist, Frans de Waal, points out (in *Good Natured*) that, if emotion-based factors, rather than rational ones, are chosen as fundamental to apparently human enterprises like morality, then there are other mammals who can have moral motivation. And there are plenty of all-too-human concepts of ethics (especially since Kant) maintaining that good and bad, right and wrong (moral values and moral behaviors) arise from the inner motives of the agent or actor, rather than from the external results of his or her actions. One of those ethical systems is called Christianity.

In an article accompanying research published by other scientists in *Nature* - research showing that chimpanzees have "cultures" too - de Waal observes that

> *all in all, the evidence is overwhelming that chimpanzees have a remarkable ability to invent new customs and technologies, and that they pass these on socially rather than genetically.*

Distinctive cultural transmission, feelings, instincts... what else do at least some animals have to offer human beings as a model for behavior? Well, even to *recognize* any other person's or any other animal's motive or intention may not be possible *without* a well-developed sense of intuition! It might turn out that whoever has honed the sharpest instrument of intuition is the morally fittest, or at least, the most capable of making sound moral moves, with or without language as you and I know it.

Even assuming that animals such as whales do not understand English (though the chimp Washoe learned sign language and taught it to her daughter, too), can you and I understand the song of the humpback? Did you know there is evidence that humpback whales sometimes sing their songs in rhyme? According to Roger Payne (in *Among Whales*), they seem to do this especially when the musical themes are intricate, perhaps requiring mnemonic devices, just like humans do. The whale "song poems" change and change again, heard only by beings who can hear them oceans away.

If we comprehend humpbacks even less than they comprehend us, how do we know that they are not performing Bach-like compositions, where harmony is a unique tension between very old musical styles handed down through the generations and very new ones created by the individual composer? The ocean might be a place somewhat like the region of outer space known as a "libration point," which is situated at a precise spot between competing gravitational pulls of huge objects like the Earth and the moon (from the Latin *librare*, to balance, as in Libra.) There, right there, the balancing and the tension resulting from extremes are one and the same.

An event like that occurring in the ocean could produce more than melodies. Humpback songs, "like human language, appear to have a hierarchical structure," according to a *Discover Magazine* report (June 1999, p. 32). The film *Star Trek IV: The Voyage Home* portrays how understanding and respecting Humpback communication is a clue to preserving the Earth's environment, literally.

Perhaps it will be said that we humans at least can memorize better than animals can. Yet, how well can *you* recite a long and intricate song or poem? Can you remember better or communicate better than an elephant, with its infra-sound sonic messages to fellow family members over two miles away? - messages too low in frequency for humans to hear. Nonetheless they exist.

And even if we humans are able to *intuit* as well as other animals, we cannot, on our own, broadcast music over distance like those whales, send unaided messages like an elephant, perceive ultra-violet like the mantis shrimp, hover precisely in the air like a hummingbird, dive silently through the air like a hawk, signal like an individual bat, navigate as accurately as a fish, sing as clear as a lone thrush, dance as purposefully as a pheasant, wait as patiently as a cat, organize socially as well as a wolf, bond as loyally as any dog, or play as constantly as a dolphin does - just for the sheer joy of it.

OK, I know we are in the new millennium, which means we are all very busy and practical (as if all these animals were not!). You want practical? How about sonar, which humans learned from whales and bats? But the research at the Defense Advanced Research Projects Agency (DARPA) is even more practical when it comes to utilizing the real *Teh* of animals; paraphrasing from *Time* magazine (June 21, 1999), these three groups of animals or their cousins play an especially important role in the story of my lawn and me:

> *Honeybees: seeking pollen, they might be able to help find land mines when they carry tell-tale mine chemicals back to their hive.*
> *Parasitic wasps: capable of learning to detect chemical compounds, they might be trained to lead to hidden stores of chemical and biological weapons.*
> *Giant sphinx moths: males being extremely sensitive to the pheromones given off by females, they might be able to learn to detect very low levels of dangerous chemicals.*

On a less practical note, recently some Dutch researchers discovered antifungal proteins in the honey of honeybees who sip the nectar of the purple flowers of heather. Let's hope those are not the same proteins as the land-mine tracers.

Would DARPA (the successor to ARPA, as in "Arpanet," the original Internet) also be interested in researching how the ants in my front yard manage to build their homes so fast and so efficiently?

> *All things come to life, but we cannot see their source. All things appear but we cannot see the gate from which they come. All men value the knowledge of what they know, but really do not know. Only those who fall back upon what knowledge cannot know really know. Is this not a great problem? One must leave it alone and yet one cannot go anywhere without meeting it. This is what the philosophers call "It is so, I think. Or isn't it?"*
> (Chuang Tzu)

There is a third side of life with which most of our

human languages have not yet caught up, though it has always been with us and with many other living beings. Once, in a logic class many years ago, the professor asked a very scientific student to respond to the idea that, some day in the future, computers will work with more than just "1's" and "0's," and will thus no longer be digitally bound by either/or values or binary digits - what Merton called the "Yes and No."

The student said that such third-value logic is impossible, because a microchip (or whatever the gizmo was back then) can only have on or off states, thus only 1 or 0, thus building up the binary chain of computer logic. But there *is* another choice, said the professor, even from the mechanical point of view: unplug the computer.

This is not merely being coy or clever, because a Taoist view of the nature of "information" would focus on what is *not* happening or not even there! That is, as the information theorist Gregory Bateson articulates so well, it's the *difference* between things (or digits) that we must note and discriminate, not those things themselves. While things by themselves are indeed facts, they do not bring actual information until we understand or perceive how those facts differ from one another. And that opens up whole new possibilities for how we might accomplish that.

For instance, creatures who can empathize and respond emotionally to other living things can just unplug for awhile, allowing intuition to come to third-value conclusions that the machine in us knows not. It may not be possible to live without our wonderful thinking machine, but it may also not be possible to live to the fullest without intuition.

As I have already mentioned, in 18th-century Europe the Moral Sense school was a powerful force for third-value ethics. Only recently has this influence been recognized alongside John Locke and natural rights theory as a cornerstone of the philosophy of many of our country's founding fathers... and thus of the United States itself. Thomas Jefferson, for one, holds that our most basic moral values are "innate," from "instinct," and that "the moral sense is as much a part of our constitution [maybe he also meant Constitution?] as that of feeling, seeing, or hearing." This, of course, also means the moral sense is "natural" as well as universal. This is another side of Jefferson, one rarely seen by Americans today. The Enlightenment was not lit by reason alone.

But what I call third-value ethics has yet to be really developed. The consequences of opening up our value systems to new alternatives are as yet unknown. Immanuel Kant himself hints at this when his theory of the universalizable Categorical Imperative leads him to come to such ethical conclusions as this: "We can judge the heart of a man by his treatment of animals." And a contemporary philosopher, Gilles Deleuze (who died in 1995), takes that thought even farther: the heart of a human being or even the essence of being human lies in our ability to rise above (or sink below) our humanity. That does not sound so paradoxical when we understand and empathize with non-human beings.

We humans have the capacity to strengthen the heart by using and perfecting our common moral sense, by relying more on empathy and intuition. With the aid of imagination we can refine that moral sense far beyond its current, idle state, though that can happen only if we guard against the economy's co-opting of imagination as just one more sales tool (or product) - witness Rolf Jensen's 1999 book, *The Dream Society* (McGraw Hill), with it subtitle, "How the Coming Shift from Information to Imagination will Transform your Business."

In fact, we might want to imitate - or just imagine imitating - the animals other than ourselves, for they have transformed the senses we share with them far beyond the limitations of human experience. But not beyond the borders of the human heart.

The Spirit of Logic

Logic Exists Too

No matter how significant or deep any "non-rational" capacities and visions may be, the issue of what it means to be rational affects all discussions of both human and non-human life. Moreover, as we have seen, defending the non-rational is not the same as defending the irrational. There are excellent evolutionary (as well as philosophical) reasons for avoiding domination by emotional, sexual or other appetites. On this the ancient and modern Greeks, Jews, Christians, Mayans and Taoists surely all agree.

In our Western cultural traditions, rationality is best exemplified by the study of logic, especially modern mathematical logic, the field that I was studying in that college class on computer logic. But over half a century ago, formal logic changed as much as physics did, yet almost no general reader, of whatever educational level, knows this crucial fact.

When mathematical logic, physics, and astronomy all point increasingly in the same strange direction, it is time to figure out the common force behind this development, which is represented poetically as:

Logic exists
for it stands
no proof,
to prove itself
it must
negate itself.

(Anya Fisher, *Human Nature...*
A Grammatical Mistake,
Remo Publishers, 1978)

Let's think like Aristotelians for once, and ask ourselves: What does it mean to be "rational"? On the popular level, we have already come upon the standard answer - to be rational is to behave in moderation. To behave in excessive ways, in turn, is to be irrational, or at the very least, non-rational.

Of course there are other popular answers, some of which we have already noted. To be rational may point to the capacity for coherent speech, possessing a soul, the tendency to pray and hope, or just to be self-conscious.

But on the technical level of logic, "rational" has a more sophisticated tradition. In this more academic use, mathematical logicians have dealt with rationality by defining it in terms of what is provable. Lewis Carroll (Charles Dodgson), in real life an obscure teacher of symbolic logic, deals with rationality by making fun of it in *Alice's Adventures in Wonderland* and *Through the Looking-Glass*. On one level these are two classic children's stories and, on another, logical parodies and corny jokes about the limitations of logic.

In the first volume, Alice is talking with the Cheshire Cat. The Cat indicates the direction to get to the Hatter and the March Hare.

> *"Visit either you like: they're both mad," said the Cat.*
> *"But I don't want to go among mad people," Alice remarked.*
> *"Oh, you can't help that," said the Cat: "we're all mad here. I'm mad. You're mad."*
> *"How do you know I'm mad?" said Alice.*
> *"You must be," said the Cat, "or you wouldn't have come here."*
> *Alice didn't think that proved it at all; however, she went on: "And how do you know that you're mad?"*
> *"To begin with," said the Cat, "a dog's not mad. You grant that?"*
> *"I suppose so," said Alice.*
> *"Well then," the Cat went on, "you see a dog growls when*

THE LAST WORLD 131

it's angry, and wags its tail when it's pleased. Now I growl when I'm pleased, and wag my tail when I'm angry. Therefore I'm mad."

Mad indeed, but not illogical!
Now let's look at what "rational" means (or used to mean) from the point of view of traditional formal or mathematical systems:

Any rational statement or idea is consistent with others, meaning it does not contradict them.

Any rational system or theory is complete; in other words, it contains all the relevant truths, theorems or conclusions within it.

These are our starting points. Let's see where they take us and what they mean for us today.

The past one hundred or more years have witnessed the gradual chipping away at the Western foundations of rationality. All of us have heard this repeatedly. Though many people are aware of some of this anti-rationalist activity, they are usually familiar with the *ir*rationalist attack, typified by existential novelists and philosophers like Jean-Paul Sartre and Albert Camus. These thinkers see reason as leading us toward nihilism, the absence of all fundamental values. If we doubt the very value of reasoning in our lives, then ultimately all of Plato's and Aristotle's "essences" or definitions disappear, leaving each of us alone in the universe with only our own bare existence.

But there is another tradition, which I have been calling non-rationalist as opposed to irrationalist. This tradition was pioneered by firm believers in reason and formal logic, who nonetheless were forced to come to certain conclusions that made them question their own assumptions about what rationality is.

The two main assumptions they made are the ones

given above: consistency and completeness. Of course, most logicians speak to each other, not to the public, and do not use the popular phrases I am using here, such as "rational." But the meaning is the same, and to speak in pure formal or metaformal symbology would end up being useless as well as boring for general readers.

Actually, the biggest discovery in modern mathematical logic can best be understood as a mystery story: like clues at a murder scene being fit into the process of drawing conclusions, the evidence left is highly technical (understood by chemists, pathologists, forensic experts and lawyers). Yet anyone can comprehend the broad outlines of the detective's thinking process as he or she concludes who is the most likely suspect, his or her motive, and the mode of operation. In both cases there is a logic of discovery.

Waiting for Gödel

The high point of my college experience was the year of mathematical logic I took when I worked on my Ph.D. in philosophy, and the semester on "undecidability" was the most difficult, most rewarding intellectual effort I have ever made. Perhaps the most readable, detailed description of the importance of this realm of thought is a number of Roger Penrose's works, especially *Shadows of the Mind* (Oxford U.P.: 1994). More recent is *Gödel: A Life of Logic*, by John L. Casti and Werner DePauli (Perseus, 2000), also clearly written and with biographical background.

I wrote an article published way back in 1978 that attempted to explain Gödel's great discovery to an unlistening world. Such is the fear of anything that looks like mathematics that most educated people have not even heard about the adventure they are missing. It ranks with relativity theory and quantum mechanics in its revolutionary impact.

Ask yourself if you have a clue about *Time* magazine's Greatest Mathematician of the 20th Century - actually Gödel is probably the Greatest Logician Since Aristotle, but that difference is part of our mystery story.

First, what was this big discovery made in modern logic? To understand it, we have to ask a seemingly ridiculous question about logic, the formal study of reasoning: What's wrong with a contradiction? Why is it a mistake to say, for instance, "I'm happy" and "I'm not happy" at the same time and in the same sense?

You and I, mathematicians and logicians all know that this sentence about happiness can indeed be meaningful in many situations: as psychological insight, as humor or as an ironic statement indicating something other than what it seems to. But if you use the words in the sentences "I'm happy" and "I'm not happy" in exactly the same sense and in the context of trying to inform someone of something, then you are talking in contradictions.

So what? Why can't we speak in contradictions and still be good at reasoning - that is, at giving relevant reasons or evidence for the conclusion we want people to accept? The reason for ruling out contradictions is this: from any contradiction we can logically infer any sentence, formula, theorem, or conclusion. If a step of our reasoning is contradictory, that step leads endlessly down to any other sentence; not illogically or psychologically, but logically and rigorously.

So the statements "I'm happy" and "I'm not happy," in a reasoning situation, leads to such statements as "The moon is made of cheese" and even "Cheese is made of the moon." To avoid logically concluding these false and even misleading statements, we have to rule out contradictions anywhere in our reasoning process.

Looking at this whole question more generally, we can see that any logical system must be consistent; it must be without contradictions if it is to be useful to us. But if it is consistent, then it cannot include all possible statements or formulas. By contrast, if we do have a contradiction in our system, we can conclude any other statement at all. In other words, a contradiction logically leads to any merely grammatical statement whatsoever - and then the system is automatically complete... it would include all "well-formed formulas."

The great intellectual discovery was to prove that any *consistent* logical system (of an order of complexity of arithmetic or greater) is necessarily *in*complete. The only way such a system could be complete would be through the unproductive route of first rendering it inconsistent.

The sleuth who solved the mystery of rationality was the young Kurt Gödel. In 1931, he published a paper proving that a consistent logical system of sufficient complexity - computer logic would be our example nowadays - *must* be incomplete. Let's see how he accomplished such a feat, which really amounts to logic proving its own limitations.

Here I will only outline the elegance of Gödel's Proof. Suppose we have a consistent formal system that can generate the system of numbers we all know so well. Sooner or later, Gödel shows, we will come across a formula that is true and yet undecidable: neither it *nor* its negation can be proven by our system. Perhaps some other system could prove this formula, but that would be a different system and would have its own undecidables... its own problems.

Carried to its extreme, Gödel's Proof is the proof that some true formulas cannot be proved to be true! Strange as this may sound, the Proof logically demonstrates that *some* truths cannot be logically demonstrated.

This means that a computer, no matter how powerful, is inherently limited in what it can compute. A few years after these seminal ideas were published, they helped inspire Alan Turing to found the field of computer science. If logic is limited by itself, Turing reasoned, so is the computing function of the human brain and any machine constructed to compute like the brain does.

Incompleteness is the price we pay for real information. But while this rules out the typical sci-fi nightmare of the omniscient computer controlling our every move, it leaves us with a lesson about ourselves.

This is because people too are logical beings, at least in part. Whenever we try to prove, conclude, or argue for or against a proposition, we are in our logic mode. In these cases we can learn about ourselves from our imperfect creation, the computer. Is it possible for people to deduce and so discover their own limits? Could we not use this logical side of ourselves as a guide and refrain from acts and fantasies that are beyond our limits of doing and suffering?

Walking Home with Gödel

However, Gödel's Proof goes way beyond the mystery of the individual and his reasoning limits. Gödel's point applies across the board for *any* formal system which is logically powerful. Physics, for example, simply cannot prove all physical truths - that is logically impossible.

So much, then for some aspiring physicists' dream to create an all-encompassing Grand Unified Theory, explaining all physical forces in one set of formulas, and applying to the smallest particle in the atom as well as to the largest clusters of galaxies. Such a complete physical theory would have an inconsistency. Something (even though true) has to be left out in order for it to retain its consistency.

Gödel himself later worked on the biggest problems of physics. I have referred not only to quantum issues but also cosmological questions like the Big Bang. That has to be a metaphor because it wasn't literally big or noisy since there was no one around to perceive it - unless Berkeley is right that it must have been perceived by some being or other in order to have existed at all!

Anyway, a Gödelian approach might say that the whole universe, if "it" is itself consistent, is also incomplete, expanding "forever" like an arithmetic progression, "$n + 1$ more," without anything out there to stop it. Poe's "Never More" becomes "Always More".

In a similar way, it is time to admit that no one psychological theory can reveal all truths about human feelings or behavior. So beware of any such theory or therapy that claims to be both logical and all-encompassing. On the other hand, don't blame a psychological theory for not being able to cover every conceivable issue or illness. More than one approach is likely to be called for.

Not that all theories in all fields try to be formally correct or logical. They may not proceed from axioms or assumptions to conclusions in even a casual manner. Those that do not pretend to be formally logical are exempt from Gödel's detective work - they cannot be proven wrong, but that comes at the price of not being provable as correct, either. Religious and poetic approaches to intuition are in this category, but while we must see their contributions in a limited light, that light is more necessary and radiant than most of us had assumed to be the case in the current and future century of science, computers, and technological progress.

The lesson of modern logic seems to be that the cement of all rationality is consistency, and that does not mix with completeness. When an idea that is as central to our lives as rationality turns out to depend on incompleteness, when rationality seems to be denuded of every characteristic except simple consistency, then it is high time to look carefully again at our rational side.

We must ask the right questions of the human mind, just as Gödel asks of logic. In the words of Francine du Plessix Gray in her study of the mind of the Marquis de Sade, we must "probe the mystery of human incompleteness."

And Casti and DePauli (above, p. 3) quote the Austrian

economist Oskar Morgenstern on the human mystery that was the late, great Kurt Gödel:

Indeed, eminent thinkers... have declared that he is definitely the greatest logician since Leibniz, or even since Aristotle... Einstein once told me that his own work no longer meant much to him, and that he simply came to the [Princeton] Institute [for Advanced Study] to have the privilege of walking home with Gödel.

The Mill Stone

You may recall that I promised or threatened to tell still another personal story about my less-than-conscious battles to counterbalance my own extremes in ideas and emotions. Certainly studying formal logic was an extreme but very positive experience for me. But at another Ivy League graduate school that I attended briefly before moving elsewhere to study formal logic and earn my Ph.D., first-year students had to take a one-time exam; ours was to be on John Stuart Mill's *A System of Logic*, an obscure work of interest only to historians of logic and the philosophy of science.

When I wrote my answers, I attacked Mill's basic assumption rather than his logical system: I pointed out what I thought was a lesson of then-contemporary physics. Mill's major assumption was that "The future will be like the past." That's it. He was perfectly aware of his own assumption and as sure of it as my high-school geometry teacher was of the Parallel Postulate.

The distinguished chairman of the philosophy department was furious. He called me in and said that anyone who would question Mill's premise (without even the decency or perhaps the reasoning ability to critique the details of his system itself) would probably not survive in his department. He would allow me one more chance by taking another exam on another topic, but failure at that would mean I would be asked to leave the graduate program.

Seeing the writing on the wall (and some that was not visible there), I decided I would quit the program (why in the world should I be grist for his Mill?), but this meant I would miss the next exam, which was to be on David Hume. This, the very same Hume who questioned our most fundamental assumptions about what we are quite sure we know! The eminent chairman did not notice the irony. Even funnier, Hume is the same philosopher I chose a couple years later as the subject of my Ph.D. dissertation at another university.

This is a good example of both my attempt to stick with my own extreme tendencies and the modern questioning of the premises of reason itself. The point was not that *I* was correct and the chairman wrong - I am not even clear how this could be decided - but that I did continue (as Hume would have wanted) to question Mill's ultimate assumption in the face of academic ridicule severe enough to make me feel shame in spite of myself for years... in fact, until 1974, when I first came upon Robert Pirsig's very similar experiences, at a different university, as recounted in his *Zen and the Art of Motorcycle Maintenance*.

On the other hand, had I stayed around and fought the good (though futile) fight, my self-counterbalancing might have ended up clear of such shame, replaced perhaps merely by the feeling of failure or - who knows? - even of a weird success.

But then, of course, I would not have gone on to study systems of modern logic which, even before Mill wrote his own, were supplanting the old assumptions and axioms, his included.

Now let's look at Mill's first axiom: The future will be like the past.

But right away we notice that the "future" is not a thing, much less something we can compare to the "past," which is also not a thing. Even if we could cut up Time that way, traditional logic would say that we cannot know that which has not occurred yet, and what we do know about the past is uncertain, unclear and often controversial.

Metaphorically speaking, then, the past and the future are subject to incompleteness if they are included in our system of rational logic.

Perhaps this is why a profoundly intuitive philosopher like Henri Bergson or a strangely imaginative writer like Proust can tell us more about the past and perhaps the future than Mill could ever guess. Great French minds are not constrained by the bounds of logic at all.

Over the past century, as we have seen, it is reason itself that has limited reason. Logic has circumscribed logic. As Mill's Utilitarian predecessor, that same Hume, had foreseen, when that happens we need to be ready with an alternative behavior... an approach that is not irrationalist (denying any substantive role to logic), that allows logic to prosper in its proper realm, and that encourages both scientific rigor and religious, poetic and "nature" feelings and intuitions.

Logic is embedded even in the language you and I speak and write every day, whether English or French or the like, specifically in its syntax. But we are fortunate indeed to have poetic minds around who make sure that our intuitions, instincts, hunches, and feelings balance out Mill's type of rationalism: e.e. cummings goes so far as to say

> *since feeling is first*
> *who pays any attention*
> *to the syntax of things...*

The River Calls

The Good Ship

That incompleteness and rationality go hand in hand also lends credence to the attempt of the human mind to build ethical guidelines for our behavior. No longer can an ethical system be faulted for not covering any and every conceivable case. In fact, an ethical and rational system can be faulted just for claiming to be so general that no real-life case can escape its principles.

Yet, we now know that if those principles pretend to proceed logically from clear assumptions and definitions to conclusions about what to do or not to do, they cannot cover every possible scenario. That is their logical strength, not their ethical weakness.

So a rational ethics is self-limiting; and a non-rational ethics is not open to demonstration as either true or false. It is now time to look at the "digitizing" of ethics - moral principles of action and of judgment caught between two dualistic values that preclude any other options.

Previously, Thomas Merton showed us how the "Yes" and "No" of everyday life, like the other Western-style dualisms, constrain us inside our minds. Our learned response is to try to protect our freedom of choice by circling the wagons around us - the moral values, the judgments of right and wrong.

This is another key characteristic of Western morality. As such, it is essentially an abstract response, like Hui's in Merton's rendering of the Taoist poem quoted above, in contrast to Taoist intuition, or to the Zen-like oneness of the chooser and the chosen, or to the mysticism of the Arhuaco people of Colombia's Sierra Nevada. According to a *Washington Post* on-site report on the Arhuaco, for them

There is no heaven or hell; everything, however spiritual, is here on earth and connected to everything else. There is no distinction between good and evil as modern Americans and Europeans understand it; things are either in harmony with nature or not.
(October 11, 1992, p. A8)

Nevertheless, even our language, as we know all too well, separates good from evil, among many dichotomies. And to grapple with that reality of our culture, we need logic and we need to be good at using it. As I have previously indicated, in recent years no Western Wayfarer has grappled with "values" as logically and as thoroughly as Robert Pirsig, whether inside a slow-moving graduate school or astride a speeding motorcycle.

My own struggle to get more time and space - and my current, very pressing choices on how to survive economically while actually enjoying these dimensions of life - are minor skirmishes compared to the value wars carried on by Pirsig, his alter ego Phaedrus (in *Motorcycle Maintenance*) and Phaedrus' own alter ego, the captain of the sailing yacht in Pirsig's second book, *Lila*. With your patience and indulgence, let me explain all this.

Like a 17-year locust, Pirsig transmogrified from "values" to "morals," that is, from metaphysical issues to ethical issues, between the first creation and his most recent book.

In *Motorcycle Maintenance*, Pirsig/Phaedrus is a "fix-it" artist when it comes to motorcycles, especially street bikes. But one of the other characters in the book was a biker who refused ever to repair his own machine. We have all met this type of person: plumbers whose home kitchen faucets are always dripping; doctors who smoke and drink and generally ignore their own health; environmentalists who mail millions of inadequately recycled, tree-consuming letters soliciting funds to save the trees.

Yet Pirsig sees that not all of these people are hypocrites; rather, they carry around mental assumptions that prevent them from engaging completely with their immediate world. These mental but unconscious prejudices separate the "internal" person (the subject) from "external" objects like motorcycles or trees.

A motorcycle trip (Pirsig driving, his son Chris on the back) is a very Western idea, while a river cruise (as in *Lila*) is very Eastern. The motorcycle adventure across the western United States is the setting for understanding Zen, a non-Western approach to value. The yacht trip down New York State, in the eastern part of the country, is the setting for a Western explanation of morals, in other words, a logical explanation of values imbedded in human interactions.

Because we have already looked at the first book in some respects, we will look a little closer into the second. As the taciturn author typically does not mention, "Lila" is not merely a female name; I note that it is also an ancient Sanskrit term meaning something like "play of the gods."

By the way, you will get a better feel for such play if you listen to the audio tape of *Lila*, which comes across as more free-flowing, closer to its water-borne metaphor, than the written and rather linear version.

The sailboat is carrying Phaedrus and, for part of the cruise, a lost woman of the night named Lila into and then down the Hudson River. They pass around geographical and conceptual bends and turns, over shallows and depths both real and ideal, past New York City and its submerged dangers, and finally into the Atlantic Ocean with its welcoming possibilities for wisdom.

During the cruise, two types of moral discourse occur: a theoretical type that proposes a rational evolutionary ethics; and a non-rational, practical type that forces Phaedrus to deal face-to-face with another human, not at all an abstraction but an individual woman in pain. The first type is easier for Phaedrus to handle... because it deals with logic, not emotion or intuition.

THE LAST WORLD   143

In terms of philosophical theory, Phaedrus once learned of a nonconformist Pueblo Indian in Zuñi, New Mexico, who did not fit into the Zuñi culture but who nonetheless was eventually absorbed by it to the point where he became one of its moral leaders. Whereas in his first book Pirsig would have seen this as a battle between Classic Quality (the logic of social cohesion) and Romantic Quality (creative individualism, shamanism in this case), now he sees it as static vs. Dynamic Quality. Social rules of behavior are normally static and require Dynamic people to move them forward as the whole society struggles to adapt and survive.

In terms of ethical rules, those that have more pure Quality are morally superior, according to this view. The higher the level of generality, the greater the Quality. Pirsig/Phaedrus thinks of the order of generality (conceptual inclusiveness), from lowest to highest, as: the inorganic (the physical), then the organic (the biological), followed by the social, and finally the intellectual. Only the intellectual includes all other levels.

For example, in order for us to exercise the intellect, it is necessary and therefore ethical to defend freedom of speech; thus social/legal pressures to limit or stop speech are morally wrong. On the other hand, it is ethical to restrain sexual behavior in cases where the wild biological impulses would overwhelm or even destroy our social ties to one another.

Now it becomes clear why Phaedrus the *alter ego*, not Pirsig the author, is the real narrator of the story of Lila. Phaedrus, in the first book, out-Aristotle'd Aristotle in his passion for rigorous abstraction, categorization, and logical deduction. In fact, he took logic so seriously that society regarded him as excessively rigorous and threw him into a mental institution. He had become immoderate in his thinking, period, and had to pay the price for following his golden extremes.

Outlaw Qualities

Floating down the river in his yacht many years later, Phaedrus is beginning to distinguish the two types of ethical issues: what I have called ethical theory (his logical philosophy of the four levels of expanding generality and increasing Quality); and ethical practice - interacting with other people, and in particular, with an attractive prostitute (Lila) sharing his bed and boat.

Phaedrus took his lead on the first type, the logic of ethics, from William James Sidis, an unappreciated genius living at the turn of this century. From Sidis, Phaedrus learned to distinguish the standard European ethical framework from the American Indian (Zuñi-like) approach to right and wrong - a moral approach that the white culture at first considered to be typical of outlaws.

But according to Sidis, the Native American view gradually became the American cowboy's and then became the indigenous stream flowing into the great river that is modern ethics.

As articulated by Phaedrus, these indigenous moral values were, and still are: simplicity; directness; avoidance of wasteful or ornamental expression and technology; trust of others; aggressiveness to the point of fierceness; and oneness with and deep respect for nature.

"Values" are ideals toward which we reach - purposes of our actions, what traditional linear philosophy called "teleological" causes, the end point, not the stimulus, of many actions. No person or community is ever completely successful in achieving their ideals in day-to-day life - no Christian, no American Indian is.

For example, Native Americans did not always have oneness with or respect for nature. In a *Washington Post* article (December 5, 1994, p. A3), reporter Gary Lee gives some examples such as the often-cited driving of bison over cliffs, but concludes that "such acts pale in comparison to the assaults Europeans would later launch on the continent's resources." (This article is largely a review of William MacLeish's *The Day Before America*.)

Taoism would tell us to judge these ethical theories as theories - on their ideals, not their practice.

In any case, several but not all of the original American moral values are still typical of "Americans" today. But the values listed above - especially not separating ourselves from our natural environment - up to now have been diluted by the on-rush of Europeans, quite possibly at the peril of destroying the Earth-home that indigenous philosophy regards as an organic and eternal unity.

Theory and practice, a major dualism in European eyes, do not appear antagonistic or even separate to Native Americans. Heeding this nondualistic trait of Dynamic Quality, Phaedrus tries to do the right thing in his personal relationship with Lila. Suffice it to say that this attempt is misunderstood and misinterpreted, at least by the powers of society, and therefore does not work. The power of social rules wins over empathy between two people in an intimate relationship.

It might be said that by the end of the trip, Phaedrus has moved from the rational ethics of abstraction toward the non-rational ethics of empathy. But he does not quite get there, or synthesize these two levels of ethics. He remains "digital," a mystic manqué, within a self-divided society.

Like the biblical Zophar, Phaedrus cannot suspend moral judgment long enough to feel empathy for a suffering fellow-being. This is not because Phaedrus or Pirsig are judgmental or moralistic - it is because moral judgments are the essence of human valuation itself, which in turn is the necessary predecessor of all other conclusions - moral, scientific, or any other kind.

Nevertheless, Lila, a real person, hurting to the point of being "insane" - a label you would think Phaedrus, who (as depicted in *Motorcycle Maintenance*) was himself committed and locked up, would be very sensitive about - is separated out from all of these important theoretical concerns. Ultimately she is lost among the boats and their captains.

In *Talking With Nature* (H. J. Kramer: 1987, p. 125), Michael J. Roads hears his own river say:

> *Do not look for separation.*
> *The I that calls is not separate from the I which responds. To those who are aware of their sensitivity and are determined to cultivate and encourage their finer feelings, life calls in many varied ways.*
> *For you, the river calls...*

The ancient American, less-abstract stream of philosophy is still flowing into the great Wayfaring river, and is at least as accessible to modern Americans as Taoism is. Even to suburbanites like me! Perhaps now I understand why "cowboys and Indians" have always fascinated me.

To the Sidis/Phaedrus theory of separate streams of European and indigenous American moral values, I would add a third, perhaps best represented by Hispanic/Indian ("Latin") American cultures over the last four centuries. Simon Bolivar, the liberator of much of South America from Spanish rule, states: "We are a microcosm of the human race. We are a world apart, confined within two oceans. We are neither Indians nor Europeans, but a part of each."

Chuang Tzu's "same river" (as cited by Thomas Merton) contains and sustains many ethical currents from all over the cultural globe, including European and Chinese ethical values as well as those native to America. And as Jung says in a 1930 article on "The Complications of American Psychology" (quoted by Smoley and Kinney in their *Hidden Wisdom* (Penguin/Arkana: 1999, p. 172): "the spirit of the Indian gets at the American from within and without."

Max Brand (Frederick Faust), who along with Zane Grey is our greatest Western story writer, put a lot of these contradictions and ironies together in 1930 in a strange novel, *The Outlaw of Buffalo Flat*, in which the hero, apparently a young Chinese man named Ching Wo, is a Taoist cowboy in the old West. (Seriously.) He patiently quotes Lao Tzu while applying his Indian skills of riding, tracking and knife-fighting. He is effective not only because he possesses these multiple levels of skills but also because his opponents (white or Chinese or whatever) cannot categorize him and so cannot predict his next move. Nor the "outlaw" values that drive him.

But there were many and diverse philosophical headwaters in the Americas even before Columbus so recently entered the picture.

The ancient philosophies of those whom Francis Jennings calls the founders of America (in his book of that title, Norton: 1993) - the peoples of North America, Mexico, Mesoamerica, and Central and South America - constitute a still-living option, as William James might say. But we will need to make careful logical distinctions to understand just how diverse the original American Ways really were.

We can look back in time to try to comprehend and appreciate and preserve the Ways of life which posed alternative values that, 500 years ago, suddenly threatened the European power structure, secular and religious. Contemporary American culture is not quite European or Indian, and neither completely secular nor religious. We are a mixture of all these, but we give much more explicit credit to our European biological ancestors than to our Native cultural forebears.

Symbolic of this is the way traditional history books fail to fully credit the role of an Indian woman in the success of Lewis and Clark's expedition across the western frontier in the early 1800s. Sacagawea guided them across the mountains and saved them from starvation when they met up with her long-lost Shoshone brother. The Shoshones lived in a democracy and were masterful horsemen. Without the teenage Sacagawea, Lewis and

Clark would not have returned as President Jefferson's heroic discoverers. That would have made white western expansion problematic, to say the least. Her white husband, the French (that is, European) guide Charbonneau, was of little help in finding the way west.

The expedition's more European-trained leader, Meriwether Lewis, was never able to fully reintegrate back into normal society, fell into depression and despair, and probably committed suicide at the age of 34. This brilliant former private secretary to the U.S. president was not the last person to fall into the gap between two or more different worlds of value.

Jack Kerouac (a more recent road worrier) puts it this way toward the end of *On The Road*, the classic American "beat" travel story of Pirsig's generation:

The waves are Chinese, but the earth is an Indian thing.

"Among the Clouds of the Tempest"

Discovery in America

In all the controversy - still not extinguished - leading up to the 500th anniversary of Columbus' landfall onto the Americas, most of the issues were framed in political terms. In 1992, "political correctness" insisted that we mourn and regret, not celebrate, October 12 of that year: mourn the ignorance, diseases, and slavery (including that practiced by the Spanish and other explorers, as well as by soldiers and clergy) that annihilated millions of indigenous people; and regret the rape of a pristine land that nonetheless still nurtures its modern inhabitants, the far-flung children of Columbus and Cortes.

My concern is not political but philosophical and logical. I want to understand how Columbus' worldview differed logically from that of the "Americans" he and others encountered. I ask myself, exactly how were the metaphysical and logical, theological, linguistic, political/legal, and ethical philosophies of the original Americans different from the standard Columbian views?

The tantalizing tidbits I have already mentioned - such as Maya and Cheyenne concepts of spacetime, the Zuñi Indian approach to values, the Shoshone love of democracy - are part of a highly diverse range of concepts and precepts that were developed (sometimes in written texts, as with the Maya) hundreds or thousands of years before Columbus. We should not repeat past mistakes by assuming that the "Indians" of the Americas were any more monolithic in philosophical outlook than, say, the peoples living in Europe in 1492.

In order to pin down native philosophies, let's first

recall the standard worldview assumed by Europeans of Columbus' time and social background. Then we can contrast that with the conceptual structures that Columbus and others encountered in the new world, even if the philosophically unsophisticated explorers themselves could not and did not recognize these structures for what they were.

Elements of the Columbian Mind

The main features of the dominant European philosophy in 1492 included: Aristotle's theory of existence or what we have ever since called metaphysics, as well as his method of logic; the dominant Christian religion; Latin and related languages; Greek-Roman political and legal ideals; and the ethics of individual acquisitiveness.

Of course, the Europeans' Bible displayed no awareness of the existence of the Americas, and Aristotle had declared "the torrid zone" of the world uninhabitable. So these two authorities over European thinking could not realistically prepare the conquistadors and the missionaries for what they stumbled onto in the New World. Nonetheless, the souls of the native peoples were in the hands of Christians and their bodies in the hands of Aristotelians, like the doctors who were trained at Padua's medical school, where they had to swear to defend Aristotle's authority.

If we were here in 1500, and had both foresight and hindsight, we would notice the following:

Aristotelianism: Existence is dualistic. All that is real is ultimately and permanently divided into incompatible dichotomies. As we have already seen, examples are form and substance, mind and body, spirit and nature, true and false. Today, we know these dichotomies through the rigorous use of binary logic, especially in our own creation - that modern chip off the old block, the digital computer.

Whether "either/or" logic has molded European metaphysics or vice versa is hard to say, but in any case Aristotle - who 500 years ago was known simply as The Philosopher, history's single most important thinker in the eyes of Europeans - established both of these fields as dualistic.

Christianity: The Roman Catholic Church rules over the interpretation of the martyrdom of Jesus as well as the ultimate meaning of Aristotle. Baptism and other sacraments mark the spiritual progress of the eternal and individual human soul, considered as separate from any physical progress made by the human body in its too-short lifetime.

Language of names: The European tongues separate nouns from verbs and from adjectives. Names stand for or symbolize discrete, independent objects in time and space "out there."

Greek-Roman ideals: Political and legal systems are top-down, pyramid-like, male-ruled hierarchies, and our place in them depends on the private property we own or control.

Individualistic ethics: Living is but a battle - with poverty, disease, war, and the threat of hell in the afterlife - that can be won only by each person acquiring more food, goods, sex, and information than competitors have.

Of course, in any of these five elements of the Columbian mind, we could find parallels to indigenous views. Dualism, for instance, was also active in certain regions of the Americas. And an ethic of competitiveness and individual wealth characterized the cultures of the northwest coast of North America, as symbolized by the potlatch - conspicuous acquisition and consumption as a means to higher status and greater power over others. But the *combination* of all the above elements at that time was uniquely European.

From the Americas come the following pre-Columbian contrasts to the five elements of Columbian thought-patterns around the year 1500.

Richard Spiegel

The Maya Way

This is how the Maya alternative to Western metaphysics and logic is treated in a classic text of our culture, H. G. Wells's *The Outline of History*. In Book III, the celebrated author states, in regard to the pre-Columbian civilizations, that on the one hand they

> may ultimately prove of very great help to our understanding of human development, because they seem to have preserved... ideas and methods that passed out of Old-World experience five or six thousand years B.C.
> (Doubleday, p. 153)

In taking a specific case, on the other hand,

> It is as if the Maya mind had developed along a different line from that followed by the Old-World mind, had acquired a different twist to its ideas, was not, indeed, by Old-World standards a strictly rational mind at all.

So far, fair enough. But Wells the European goes much farther, and links "these aberrant American civilizations to the idea of a general mental aberration... " Such is the traditional portrayal of the pre-Columbian mind.

Actually, as I hinted above, the Maya were a real potential threat to Columbian metaphysics - and still are, whether in Wells's time early last century or now in the 21st - wherever the Columbian has not been superseded by a cogent post-Columbian metaphysics. In other words, Aristotle had theoretical competition in Central America - until Cortes crushed it temporarily beneath iron spears and horse shoes. I say "temporarily" because the Maya of today's Mexican Yucatan and parts of Honduras and Guatemala have still not given up. Their first civil war, with the early conquistadors, lasted 150 years. A drop in the bucket, according to the Maya concept of time.

The Maya appear to us now to have grasped not only

the *infinity* of cosmic time within a *cyclical* metaphor (like the corn cycle), but also the significance of *historical time* (commencing in what we now designate 3133 B.C.E.), where *human beings* are the actors, scientific observers, and religious prognosticators.

The Maya, like the Hopi, tell us this is the last human-based cycle, and time is running out.

The Maya, as we have noted, wrote books on paper-like materials collected in libraries, almost all of which were systematically destroyed by the devil-extirpating Europeans. In Wells's defense, I should mention that this written language has only recently been deciphered. We now know that the Maya were mathematical astronomers light-years ahead of their European contemporaries. This is even aside from León-Portilla's insight (discussed above) that they probably did not divide space from time or science from religion.

Through an advanced science, Maya studies and records of calendrical time were simultaneously initiations into mystical experience. Astronomical predictions of planetary movements - often projected over millions of years - were at the same time prophecies of the actions of the gods. Pyramid-observatories were also centers for the study of the forces behind human events. As science became religion, the object became the subject and the individual the infinite.

This logic of merging, though very different from Europe's early scientific method, was the foundation of Maya science, as we are now learning and as Wells could not have known.

One aspect of their logic, the Maya's vigesimal number system (base 20), is an advanced computational system - more complex in some ways than our decimal system. More importantly, the Maya worked with three place values (1, 5 and 0), compared to our digital logic (1/0, or yes/no, or on/off) and that of our dualistic computers, which as we have seen were created in our own Western image. Mayan logic irrational? Aberrant? Not any longer: it just took a while for the Western mind to catch up with it, though it still hasn't in some ways.

With its metaphysics of oneness, the Maya concept of order was based not on logical categories but on cosmic purpose, facilitated by human understanding and social participation. However, it was made possible by third-value concepts - so difficult for thinkers within Aristotle's tradition.

But if Yes, in our Western view, never turns into No, from Taoism we learn that Yin can become Yang and vice versa, opening up unknown third possibilities that are a threat to the established powers-that-be.

Why is that? Because the masses are easier to control when they think they have few options - which, in fact, is all they do have whenever thinking itself is limited to just two-ness. If "mental aberration" stands for mental illness, and if the latter can be viewed as the condition of having too-few options for taking action, then it was the dualism-bound Europeans who were the true aberrants of the new world.

The Aztec Religious Challenge

The Popes gave the Spaniards permission to possess the new lands, which became literally private property for the first time. One reason for this grant, aside from the politics of the day, may have been the threat of a conceptual alternative to medieval Christianity as symbolized by the theology of the Aztecs in the Valley of Mexico. Church leaders were as concerned to prevent this New World gospel from spreading as they were to save Aztec (and other native) souls from hell.

As justified by the Aztecs' sacrificing of their enemies to their many gods, Cortes' destruction of the ancient Mexican civilization just happened to coincide with the rise of anti-Catholic challenges to papal authority in

Europe. Aztec theology, like the domestic European challenges to the Church, emphasized, first, the opposition of good vs. evil, such as the battle between the creator god Quetzalcoatl - as uniquely bearded, armored and abrupt in appearance as Cortes himself - and evil forces; and second, the absence of individual free will.

Such dualistic determinism (which is a healthy reminder, as well, of the philosophical diversity of the Americas at the time) reminds us of the early Protestants, minus the polytheism and blood sacrifice, both of which appear to have been equally offensive to Quetzalcoatl.

Yet Christians of whatever kind were much more horrified by the removal of a still-beating heart in Mexico than the torture of a still-breathing "witch" back home. In contrast to the Christian concern with the purity and salvation of the individual soul,

> *the Aztec religion was one of propitiation. The individual worshipper was not striving for spiritual perfection or personal salvation, but was trying to influence the natural forces so that they worked in his favour or for the good of the community as a whole.*
> (Warwick Bray, *Everyday Life of the Aztecs*, Peter Bedrick Books: 1968, p. 152)

One of the few fictional approaches to this Aztec concept is D. H. Lawrence's *The Plumed Serpent*. The title's reference is to Quetzalcoatl. W. Y. Tindall, in his introduction to the first Vintage International Edition of the novel (which was originally published in 1926), observes:

> *Bird and snake together, this Aztec god expresses not only a Freudian vision but that connection of earth and sky, matter and spirit, above and below which thrice-great Hermes commended.*
> (Introduction, xi)

This is a reference to "Hermes Trismegistus," the legendary founder or founders (perhaps Egyptian) of the Hermetic mystical tradition in the West - an even more profound challenge to the Church of the day, because that mysticism was mostly home-grown and gradually mixed with the Jewish Cabala and alchemy as the most durable occult tradition in European civilization.

In the novel, Don Ramon thinks of himself as both serpent of the earth and bird of the sky: "I am lord of two ways," he says; "I am master of up and down." It was only by leaving Europe for a while and staying in New Mexico and Mexico itself that Lawrence was able to verbally paint this picture of a new and alternative world.

The Hopi Linguistic Option

"Hopi is a language that belongs to the Shoshonean branch of the Uto-Aztecan language family. Thus Hopi is related to... many language groups in central Mexico" (Taylor, *The Native Americans*, pp. 41-42). Earlier in this century, B. L. Whorf studied the structure of the Hopi language and concluded that it represented a conceptual contrast to languages such as English, which derive from Latin and related origins.

The Hopi language expresses ongoing events rather than denoting things: verb-like phrases, not nouns, dominate, and the world is expressed as a changing realm of unified activities in nature, not as a description of objects separated from the speaker. As the contemporary Hopi poet Ramson Lomatewama graphically says in *Silent Winds* (Badger Claw: 1987, "Cloud Brothers"):

For we   are truly different
and yet
we   are truly the same.

It is doubtful that Coronado understood this subtlety

when he first met up with the Hopi early in the 16th century. Indeed, the functions of the Hopi language differ so radically from those of Spanish or English that Whorf pointed to language itself as what creates our general view of reality, not the other way around.

Louis L'Amour, the great cowboy storyteller, wrote a full-length novel right before he died called *The Haunted Mesa* (Bantam paperback: 1987) that takes us back even before the Hopi, to the culture of their own Ancient Ones, the Anasazi pueblo people. An old Indian is quoted as saying that "there was a 'way,'... but all those who knew how to use it were gone" - but perhaps not. Whorf would say that if the Anasazi language still lives, so does their worldview, their reality. It is even possible to connect the language, and therefore the philosophies, of the Anasazi with the Maya's because of the archaeological evidence that the two peoples traded with one another.

Actually, "Anasazi" is a Navajo expression strictly translated as "Enemy Ancestor." And though the Hopi and the Navajo peoples are indeed at odds on many subjects and derive from completely separate linguistic and cultural roots, they have something profound in common with each other and with ancient Asian thinking.

As Tony Hillerman writes in one of his fascinating mystery novels that take place on the great Navajo Reservation in the Four Corners region of the U.S.:

> *Western metaphysicians might argue that language and imagination are products of reality. But in their own migrations out of Mongolia and over the icy Bering Strait, the Navajos brought with them a much older Asian philosophy. Thoughts, and words that spring from them, bend the individual's reality...*
>   *The Fallen Man* (HarperPaperbacks, 1996: p. 76)

Only today is the American Indian emphasis on process appreciated by European minds for encouraging a closer relationship to nature, and may even represent the quantum condition of the world better than English does, though not better than mathematics. One of the few thinkers in our century who tried to communicate "process" metaphysics in the English language was the British philosopher and logician, Alfred North Whitehead, but most students still cannot comprehend him.

To say (Hopi-like) "my lawn greens" or "the sky blues" or even "the bluing sky" is more scientifically accurate than to say that there is a lawn or a sky separate from me and from these colors. Western scientists, especially, have come to realize, as the Hopis did way back then, that the natural (including the human) universe - and perhaps spacetime itself - is ever-evolving.

Even our own Winnie the Pooh understands that!
On Wednesday, when the sky is blue,
And I have nothing else to do,
I sometimes wonder if it's true
That who is what and what is who.

Everyday Ways

The Iroquois Political and Legal Paradigm

Other indigenous American philosophies of life have an immediate, practical impact on people living at the start of the newest millennium. These are the realms of politics, law and ethics.

The Iroquois League or Federation posed a significant alternative to Greek and Roman political and legal values - so significant that American radicals like Tom Paine and Ben Franklin appealed to the Iroquois system as one paradigm for a democratic and egalitarian federalism.

As Jack Weatherford points out in *Indian Givers and Native Roots* (Crown Publishers), the Iroquois taught the early Americans a completely different model from what European history had furnished. Among the Iroquois, rank in political power was secondary to courageous example and oratorical persuasiveness.

The words "chief" and "emperor," foisted onto native political organizations by Europeans used to vertical hierarchy, were never appropriate to the Iroquois, a federation of five (eventually six) nations in what is now the northeastern United States, and originated as long as 600 years ago from the real or legendary founding fathers, Deganawidah and Hiawatha.

Iroquois women played a major role in society and in federal governance, especially the frequent judicial and arbitration duties when the men could not agree among themselves. Above all, public affairs were run by representatives ("sachems") elected by the people; they joined in councils to make those decisions and laws that affected everyone. Slavery was prohibited, even as the torture of enemies was highly valued and very nearly perfected.

It is no coincidence that neither Ben Franklin nor Tom

Paine was very well educated in the Greek and Latin classics, and thus were more open than other "Americans" to new paradigms of political and legal thinking. Consider, for instance, the legal implications of Paine's radical statement that "Everything of persecution and revenge between man and man, and everything of cruelty to animals, is a violation of moral duty." Words that are never read in an American history class! That's probably because they rise above both the European and the Indian standards of Paine's day... and ours.

Since European itself between 1492 and 1776 provided no living paradigms of democracy, we should look again at (literally, "re-spect") the Iroquois' contributions to our system of law and governance, now only a little over two centuries old.

Looking back, the Iroquois remind us that, just as our own political dualism of "liberal" vs. "conservative" is not so clear-cut today, so in the 18th century the Hamiltonian vs. the Jeffersonian, or Federalist vs. Anti-Federalist, were not as important to distinguish as the "hierarchical vs. participatory" matrix offered by the Iroquois paradigm. By now we have learned that there are different and equally logical concepts of legal, political, and metaphysical order, but that is a very recent lesson.

The new millennium may be starting with a still more difficult bifurcation - what Alan Ryan of Princeton University describes in another context (*New York Review of Books*, Vol. XLII, No. 3, February 16, 1995, p. 31) in this way: Is there an "order and purpose to life," or do "we live in what is ultimately a howling wilderness?"

Note the either/or choice. Wolves howl a lot but have one of the strongest orders, a rigid hierarchy, among mammals, most of whom do not howl. I believe it was the mental wilderness - what the American poet Wallace Stevens calls the "slovenly wilderness" - not the physical wildness of the native peoples, that the Europeans really feared. That is, it was the profound uncertainty, just as with physics and life itself.

The Inca Ethical Model

The Andean peoples centered in what is now Peru enjoyed an ethic of living and choosing very different from Columbus'. A less individualistic, more communal ethic prevailed. Perhaps the abundance of nutritious crops such as white potatoes, sweet potatoes, peppers, and squash made one-on-one competition less necessary.

If you were living then and there, you would notice that the Incas seem to play down private property in favor of a community-wide accumulation or surplus of common goods. Most decisions were made not on the personal but on the community level. State laws strictly enforced the rules of society. For example, at the time that the Incas welcomed Pizarro, it was against the law to be lazy.

We Americans of today are all too aware of not having an ethic (rational or nonrational) in common. We have substituted the iron horse and steel horsepower for the iron armor and the horses of the conquistadors, but are farther than ever from sharing a common ethical system.

Closer agreement on ethical values and judgments is no longer something we need to fear. Given the level of violence and crime and stress today, are we still so certain that our European inheritance of individualistic ethics is the final word on moral evolution?

Even the Europeans who made first contact here themselves looked back to ancient times, to Athens and Sparta and Rome and Jerusalem and Bethlehem, for their moral models; and indeed we now know that there is no single arrow of change, that even in biology natural selection and variation are not always step-wise or steady or predictable.

No one is saying we should go back to the Inca type of society, or that a more collectivist system, much less one that requires ritual bloodletting, is the way to go. But the individualism that all Americans cherish is in part our cultural inheritance from the conquistadors and Dominicans and Reformers and philosophers of Europe five centuries ago, and must now be tempered by what *Star Trek*'s Mr. Spock called "the needs of the many."

It is that side of our ethical balancing act that the Inca model can help us understand... and the side that was neither "discovered" nor understood by the European conquerors who followed Columbus. One after the other, each of these Westerners pursued the needs of the few, and of the one.

Cloud Beings

Walking over my lawn today, I looked up at the clouds.

With all the emphasis I have put on the differences between the Columbian and the pre-Columbian minds, let me conclude this chapter with several reveries, beginning with one of the Incas' incantations to their supreme deity. We can only imagine its concise and sonorous inflections, its sheer harmony, as our fellow human beings - the sacred mountains looming above them, the random clouds hurrying by overhead - beseech their Creator:

> *O Creator! O conquering Viracocha! Ever present Viracocha! Thou who art in the ends of the earth without equal! Thou who gavest life and valor to men, saying, Let this be a man! and to women, saying, Let this be a woman! Thou who madest them and gave them being!.. Thou who art in the high heavens and among the clouds of the tempest, grant this with long life...*
> (Edward Hyams and George Ordish, *The Last of the Incas*, Dorset Press, originally Simon & Schuster, Inc., 1963: 1990, p. 95)

According to the last of the classical Tang poets of China, quoted previously, this region is also

> *Where cloud-masses darken,*
> *And the wind blows ceaseless around ...*

"And," Wallace Stevens writes,

*the clouds flew round and the clouds flew round
And the clouds flew round with the clouds...
Yet that things go round and again go round
Has rather a classical sound.*

Of course, clouds are just clouds; they are things up there in the sky - or are they? Do they have precise form and mass? Perhaps not, and for that very reason are used more and more as metaphors to explain - not religion, not metaphysics - the physics of the atom. (Think of the cloud chamber.) "The" atom is our contemporary cloud-being, but it is no less metaphorical and approximate than the cloud-beings of the Hopis, their Kachinas, or the cloud-beings of the Tewa - their Oxua. Especially if, as some scientists now believe, the clouds above harbor bacteria that float above the Earth and well beyond its deadly human wars.

This may be our last world, the last chance for humanity, but not necessarily for bacteria.

The cloud-level of existence is beautifully described by Edwin Bernbaum in his *Sacred Mountains of the World* (University of California, 1997). But Wu Cailuan, a Taoist poet, had already observed in the early fourth century:

*My body lives in the city,
But my essence dwells in the mountains.*

Kubera, the Hindu god of wealth, resides in the city of Alaka on the summit of the sacred mountain of Kailas in the Himalayas. Even at this level of reality, clouds also serve as messengers between beings, profane or sacred. ("Profane" usually refers to money.)

(*IS*, p. 70)

From ancient Chinese and Sanskrit poetry to contemporary quantum physics, and from the classical eras of Native American cultures to our own, all humans try to make sense and order out of the chaos presented to us. Whether our attempts to gain this sort of control over our own lives must turn into the constant controlling of other people and nature is a question we contemporary Westerners will have to answer soon enough.

But many traditional Native Ways and their own distant cousin, Chinese Taoism, which so far has managed to stay out of the way of the conquistadors, answered that question a long time ago. And as the quantum physicists like to say, we must ask nature the right questions.

Some of these scientists have been asking whether molecules or even atoms themselves have "polarity," a kind of magnetic north and south pole.

But sometimes it is artists rather than scientists who come up with the more enduring answers. In *Legends of the American Desert*, Alex Shoumatoff cites D. H. Lawrence during his visit to the American Southwest in the 1920s:

> *What Lawrence admired about the Indians was that they had the "oldest religion," which he defined as "the whole life-effort... to... come into sheer naked contact, without a mediator or an intermediary... with the elemental life of the cosmos, mountain-life, cloud-life, thunder-life, air-life, earth-life, sun-life."*

(p. 18)

"The land is within," according to the poet Louis Simpson, showing a real understanding of the American West. And of the earth-life that is my lawn.

More generally, according to the American painter Charles Burchfield in 1936: "The only divine reality is the unspeakable beauty of the world as it is."

For centuries the Navajo have been chanting their healing song, known as the Blessing Way (also a theme in Hillerman's novels), which concludes with the following lines:

May it be beautiful before me
May it be beautiful behind me
May it be beautiful all around me
In beauty may I walk
In beauty it is finished.
   (Quoted in Jon E. Lewis, *The West*, Siena paperback, 1998: p. 350)

Making My Teh

Streamlining

In some other closing lines, those spoken during the rites commemorating the founding of the League of the Iroquois, it is said that, as the founders gradually pass from the scene, there will be

nothing left but a desert. There ye have taken your intellects with you.
   (William Brandon, *Indians*, American Heritage (1961), Houghton Mifflin: 1987, p. 209)

The integrity of the environment - our "immediate space" - whether that means the clouds in the sky or the high mountains or my tiny parcels of land, is connected with my own intellect and *its* integrity. The issues of my survival in spacetime and specifically of my future livelihood seem more meaningful and less self-indulgent than I had supposed. I am indeed part of a greater whole that I do not fully comprehend. I make ripples or waves in spacetime. This cannot be ignored or evaded by escaping from nature or reality, as the Taoist poet Shen Ch'uan-Ch'i forlornly seems to advocate in "The Gorges of the Yangtze":

The Magic Hill soars out of sight
Piled up in weird fantastic form.
In each ravine such shadowy night
As comes from wind and rain and storm.
In each abyss the gloom of hell
Where ghouls and hideous devil dwell.

Within the triple gorge from high

> The Moon sheds down a kind of dawn.
> In Spring the rivers nine foam by.
> What else of wild is here forlorn
> Oh! Ask not me. He who in dream
> Its spirit say would fitter seem.
> (Van Over, p. 242)

Not that the poet would have to be fearful of the gorges nowadays: the current Chinese government will soon flood them when a gigantic new $26+ billion dam is completed there. At one time the dam - China's biggest project since construction of the Great Wall itself - was only a gleam in the eye of Chairman Mao, who wrote a quite different kind of poem that included the line, "Build a stone wall in the river." Only a complete materialist could believe we can stonewall a magnificent river.

Do you recall my earlier attempts to "force" water to solve my problems with the anthills? You might think that those efforts could not be compared to the Chinese government's, but what would be the ants' point of view on that? To them the hose must have been even worse than the threat that the Three Gorges dam poses to people and other forms of life along the river.

But I must confess, just the other day I tried the water-torture again, this time on a hive of yellow-jackets that had found and occupied a hole in the wall - in the slope of the backyard, which, by the way, has just recently been taking on thick grass in loam soil protected and nourished by the lone black locust and some raspberry bushes spreading out beneath it.

So I grabbed the old hose again and, chicken that I am now in regard to wasps and bees, I rested it on the deck wall, facing their ground-home, and aimed it at the entrance. Full-force came the water as I ducked away and ran into my back door. After all, I was not about to let the swarm stay around forever, threatening not only myself but my wife and my dog.

After one hour, during which they flew around the

water in an angry buzz, I turned off the water, ran back to the safety of my house, and observed. Instantaneously, the wasps returned to their calm and organized flight patterns. As things turned out, I decided to invite the yellow-jacketed visitors to continue to use the back slope as a runway and they have never bothered anybody.

However that hive may protect itself from flooding, that is what the Chinese government should do, as opposed to storing and constraining the water with gigantic dams. Remembering *wu wei* helped me to give up and leave the yellow jackets alone. Anyway, as Chuang Tzu reminds me,

*The sound of water
says what I think.*

Given the powers and forms of nature, do I as a mere Wayfarer have *any* control over my own lawn, much less of my own life? And, as our "echoes roll from soul to soul," in Tennyson's words, do I have anything to say about my impact on other living things?

Maybe water can help me here again. Water *seems* to be something pliant, and Westerners tend to snicker a little when they hear about Taoists using water as their key metaphor in understanding nature and themselves. But we are looking through the cultural glass darkly, and the kind of experiences I have had with water in my own yard show me how tough-minded this metaphor can really be. Even some contemporary scientists and mathematicians are appealing to the characteristics of water to explain some of the common but puzzling facts around us.

For instance, when contrasting what he calls the Platonic tradition of art vs. the Taoist, an editor of the respected journal *Nature* locates the difference between these two traditions in how they "depict the most challenging of all movements: that of flowing water." Unlike most Western artists (Leonardo da Vinci being the outstanding exception), artists coming out of the Taoist tradition

have sought to capture the structures of fluid trajectories in a series of lines..., which are remarkably close to the streamlines that scientists use to depict fluid flows...
(Philip Ball, *The Self-Made Tapestry: Pattern Formation in Nature*, 1999: Oxford U.P., p. 165)

Let us now follow this trajectory. You might remember my saying that Taoism is one of the two elements of Zen Buddhism, the other being the tradition of Mahayana Buddhism. As we have seen, Wayfarers come from both the East and West, and - as with the First Americans - philosophical places in between.

For example, in *Fire in the Mind: Science, Faith, and the Search for Order* (Vintage paperback, 1996), George Johnson describes how relevant the worldview of the Tewa Indians is to the attempts by certain groups of scientists and mathematicians to understand the cosmic order. These indigenous and non-indigenous groups live and work near Santa Fe, New Mexico, which has always been one of my favorite sources of inspiration. The contrast in cultures there, like the stark landscape itself, leads different people to perceive alternative ways of organizing the same world, all of these Ways being aesthetically pleasing.

But whether objective reality (if that exists at all) conforms to one rather than another of these mental pictures is unknown and perhaps - given the way quantum physics has been going in recent decades - unknowable.

Some other Western scientists who have developed quantum theory over the past century have turned to Buddhism of one school or another - Niels Bohr is an outstanding example of a physics pioneer who believed that that Eastern Way could help him understand the unfolding if ephemeral universe inside the atom. On the "macro" level, too, spacetime as a unified continuum is perhaps the long-delayed response to Aristotle. But overturning him also has its consequences, its karma.

It is true that my own spatiotemporal imbalance could be addressed by something Eastern, like Zen Buddhist meditation (Zazen); there is nothing like it to either pivot or still the mind. But what about my original (and supposedly simpler) problem of the front and back lawns? I think of the black locust in the yard when I recall the very first Zen *koan* I ever read; I was 15 years old:

> A monk asked Joshu why Bodhidharma came to China. Joshu said: "An oak tree in the garden."
> (Paul Reps, *Zen Flesh, Zen Bones*, Anchor: undated, pp. 119-120)

    I had oak trees and gardens on my mind when I visited a Zen monastery for a few hot summer days in 1971. A slightly run-down set of buildings in the canyons of New Mexico greeted me. I learned later that the place had originally been built as a place for Roman Catholic priests to dry out from too much alcohol. But in back of the buildings there were amazing hot natural springs where you could comfortably soak and watch the clear stars at night or in the very early morning.
    As it turned out, I did a few hours of Rinzai meditation every day, but much of my time was taken up by plumbing. Yes, plumbing. A senior monk asked me the first day if I had any practical skills. I wanted to say gardening, but he would have seen through that immediately. The only thing I could think of was the summer of my 18th year, when I had helped out a master plumber, though it was hard work and not much fun. So I said that I knew a bit about plumbing. The monk's eyes went wide and shined with delight. My job, said he, would be to work with another visitor to fix the leak under the main house. I know he had his eye on me anyway, because I am not a large person and could easily fit through the narrow crawl space under the house. Which is what I did for most of two days. They say that neophytes to Zen meditation must be prepared for sore

muscles, but the esoteric technique of plumbing meditation and its karmic pains were mine and mine alone.

However, the Zen monks treated me better than they treated the person who accompanied me to the magic land of New Mexico, a professional psychologist who was too big to fit under the house and went straight into full-time Zazen, meditating in the more traditional manner for six to eight hours a day.

On the third day he asked for an audience with the abbot (also not a regular resident), who did not say a word to him but instead grabbed my friend's nose and tweaked it, with some force. At which time the psychologist, being a highly intelligent scientist, decided to leave the place. I myself fled into the wilds of the nearby forested mountains, where I could meditate in peace, for there was no plumbing out there and no leaks either.

In an article in the autumn 1992 issue of the journal *The Quest* (pp. 48-49), Ven. Joan Shikai Woodward, a Soto Zen Buddhist monk, says that

> the word "koan" means "public case," that is, a record of the direct presentation expression of practice. Language is only a metaphor for direct experience... Zen koan are not riddles to be solved, paradoxes, jokes, or locked boxes that need a key to open them. Koan are a way for learning, through experience, a whole new way of using the mind.

Or the body, I might add.

The Bodhidharma in China, the Buddha in the plumbing or in a tree, an oak in the garden or the locust tree in my yard, the yard in my community... but just where am *I* in this scheme? I am the intuiter, just one of many more or less intelligent forces at work here.

The 54th chapter of the *Tao* says that cultivating *Teh*, Virtue, in the community will make it live and grow. So to cultivate my front and backyards is to facilitate their

Virtue, allowing them to become a true garden...if I can focus my energy flow on that.

I intuit that the entire yard, front and back, still needs a lot of help - *my* help; this appears to be the *only* way to make it whole again! In fact, I am personally the vehicle of triage, through my ability to focus and commit myself to planting and encouraging the most naturally appropriate shrubs, trees, flowers, and grasses.

Above all, I think I have been right to refuse to go along with the retreating wall of erosion in back and the advancing anthills in front that threaten the whole local ecology. It is that larger picture that I need to fit into.

Streamlining my response to the lawn issues may also serve to help me with my personal and professional issues about space and time. I am afraid that my own spatial issues (such as room to enjoy fresh air and quiet) will not be resolved as easily as the erosion, nor will my temporal issues (such as frustration over time to write) be solved half as readily as getting rid of the anthills.

But in either case, to deal with one side is to deal with the other. It will take some forceful self-guiding of my energies to go ahead and make my own *Teh*, with some *wu wei* mixed in.

Heart of Earth

Now that I have decided, in the case of the yard, on a full-speed-ahead, aggressive though not all-controlling solution, I will follow the same approach to my own personal counterbalancing. For here, for now, this is my Wayfaring, my way.

Natural things can also go to extremes, can go all-out, on occasion. Recently I noticed that the big dogwood on the left upper side of the back hill had a long, dead branch stretching out to the right and close to a large grapevine cluster, and the vine had started to grow over the branch. I tucked a few more straggling vine offshoots over the dead branch - I wanted to create a bower for more privacy between my yard and the neighbor's. For a few weeks the grapevine just grew and grew until most, but not all, of the dead branch was covered. It looked like a win for us humans.

However, yesterday, I looked and could not believe what I saw. The clump of healthy, climbing grapevines had jumped ship! They had completely deserted the very dead branch and were spreading over another nearby branch, a healthy one. Not only that: the vines had obviously climbed along two very short and very dead twigs that were still attached to the old dead branch until they reached the tips of those twigs, which were barely touching the new branch. How could the vines do that? The smaller twigs, which acted as bridges from death to life, were themselves deader than their parent branch; in fact, being further from the sources of nourishment, the little bridges must have died first.

How could healthy grapevines follow dead bridges? How could they take such an enormous risk to locate life in the next, parallel branch? Or did they just *happen* to bump into a parallel, branching universe? We think of the branches of trees and vines as just things, sections of a larger something, yet they are really *patterns* - fundamental ways in which nature organizes itself.

It is clear now that I too need to know how to gracefully switch branches. In fact, I need to re-do the whole lawn of my life, because I cannot work full-time inside an office building or have my hours determined solely by other persons. Odd that these everyday expectations are the same problems American Indians have had in succeeding within the white culture!

But I will have to protect myself less for a while in order to ensure the general Quality of the remainder of my days on Earth. Risks must be taken for the sake of environmental cultivation, and the growth outcome is not assured, either for the black locust or for the grapevine or for me.

That there are also very dangerous and painful risks from taking a strong stance is shown by an incident on the edge of my front yard, that center of anthill-dom. I was mowing the steep lawn (and the ant kingdom) when I must have crossed over a hive of paper wasps (not bees) - for that is what appeared out of nowhere, first stinging the hot motor, then moving on to me, as slightly less warm. Six stung me right away, before I could run as fast as I could to the garage.

The water-hose (once again) was lying there, so I put the water full-on, trying to flush away the still-furious wasps. (I learned that day that wasps, unlike most bee life-forms, can just keep on stinging.) That did not budge them. So I took the hose itself and started knocking them off, one by one.

Now, it is true that I, a human being (and former plumber), think of myself more as an individual than as a group or modular mind, as the wasps are and the vines may be. In fact, this particular "I" traditionally denoted a very analytic, logical, organized, intellectually rigorous (though hopefully in no way rigid) person... me. All those supposed traits together make up my ego.

But some of those traits are fading a bit with time and age, as my intuitive side just gets stronger. I do hope that trend will help me find my role in the bigger pattern, of which the lawn and I are neither very significant nor insignificant elements.

Intuitively

Karma

The paths of Buddhism, including Zen, and Taoism appear to diverge at this point. For Taoism,

Neither the ego nor the rest of the phenomenal world is illusory - both are completely real.

Yet, in both paths,

The individual self is not set apart from the rest of nature but is, like all things, a product of yin and yang as the creative processes of tao.
(*Chinese Religion*, by Laurence G. Thompson, Wadsworth: 1979. 4th ed., 1989 paperback, p. 90 (both above citations)

Whatever this unfolding "I" may denote, it needs to be the one to make decisions about the design of "my" spatial environment and the time schedule of "my" work day. The fact is that almost all persons, as well as animals, living and passed from the scene, have had to spend most of their lives working for nourishment, physical and emotional.

With empathy for so many who came before me - for the Inca and for the Iroquois, for The Philosopher and for his slaves - and for those who struggle now, and who will be forced in future times to work away their lives, I now accept that "I" am no different. In the old-fashioned thinking of John Locke and Adam Smith, the labor of my mind/body mixes with the real soil of the lawn and with the hard work of other living things, humans included. That is my karma.

And what is "karma?" Cosmic justice, the overall equilibrium of the universe, all the world getting not mad but even. Karma is embodied in this true story about the lone black locust tree that is helping to hold up and hold together my back yard. The other day I noticed that still another grapevine was taking *it* over. It was a wet and foggy morning.

I placed my foot in the "V" of the tree (which, you might recall, is on the right upper side of the yard) and, wading through the now-dense raspberries and roses, hoisted myself up to chop away the vine. I slammed down the axe a couple of times, then at the next downward movement my foot slipped and I fell straight down, badly bruising my abdomen on a protruding branch - protruding sharply, because I had chopped *that* too some years ago as part of my initial grand plan to save the tree.

Karma. Glad I hadn't left the point any sharper!

In one of my oldest, favorite books, Edith Hamilton's *Mythology*, is the Greek karmic tale of Dryope, who went with her sister Iole one day to a pool to make garlands for the nymphs. Dryope was carrying her little son,

> *and seeing near the water a lotus tree full of bright blossoms she plucked some of them to please the baby. To her horror she saw drops of blood flowing down the stem. The tree was really the nymph, Lotis, who fleeing from a pursuer had taken refuge in this form. When Dryope, terrified at the ominous sight, tried to hurry away, her feet would not move; they seemed rooted in the ground. Iole watching her helplessly saw bark begin to grow upward covering her body. It had reached her face when her husband came to the spot with her father. Iole cried out what had happened and the two, rushing to the tree, embraced the still warm trunk and watered it with their tears. Dryope had time only to declare that she had done no wrong intentionally and to beg them to bring the child often to the tree to play in its shade, and some day to tell him her story so that he would think whenever he*

saw the spot: "Here in this tree-trunk, my mother is hidden." "Tell him too," she said, "never to pluck flowers, and to think every bush may be a goddess in disguise." Then she could speak no more; the bark closed over her face. She was gone forever.

The Wu *Way*

But karma does not imply that we have no say over our lives. On the contrary. By asserting some control over the hours I spend on fundraising, or working on the lawn, or writing a book on Taoism and karma, or learning more about the Maya, I will preserve more of my intellectual integrity and simultaneously get along more naturally with society. The downside, of course, is the loss of a regular paycheck. And as a "Lone Ranger" consultant, I may have to practice *wu wei* with some aspects of my money-and-politics society, which worships power over others embodied in promotions up the corporate ladder, success in the eyes of the public media, and profits competitively acquired.

As in so many other areas of life, the philosopher Friedrich Nietzsche foresaw the modern capitalist way: in *Daybreak*, he says that "The means employed by the lust for power have changed, but the same volcano continues to glow... what one formerly did for the 'sake of God' one now does for the sake of money." A somewhat more poetic take on this comes from Philip Larkin (1973):

Clearly money has something to do with life
...I listen to money singing.

Did you know that the starkly beautiful Las Vegas Valley in Nevada used to sing too, quietly, not brashly, as the springs from mountain snowmelt bubbled beneath the surface? Las Vegas is Spanish for The Meadows, and according to Timothy Egan in *Lasso the Wind: Away to the New West* (Knopf, 1998), there used to be a unique watertable there until modern greed turned it into the same desert as the rest of the Mohave. Now, the City of Las Vegas is paying homeowners $400 each to stop watering their green lawns and replace them with more appropriate landscaping of desert plants and rocks. So saving the power of water is done, if at all, not for one's family or for God or nature, but for cash. And not just in Las Vegas.

Not long ago, the normally water-full Maryland was in a serious drought, unknown to any living thing here, and it makes me wonder what the original Meadows must have looked, felt and tasted like before the casinos and the riskers-of-water took over in that part of the world.

According to wu wei, *the Way to establish yourself and what is yours lies in being promoted by the world, victory is in the spontaneous accord of the world, and gain is in having the world give it to you, not in taking it for yourself.*

(Wen Tzu, #154)

Just as a more yang-like approach to the lawn can lead to its greater receptivity (yin), likewise, my yang-like decision to purposefully cultivate the economic side of my self-balancing act may lead to a much greater use of my own powers of intuition. Indeed, over the last few years, my direct intuitions of reality - whether knowing what people are thinking or planning, or predicting political trends, or grasping what sick people need to get well - have been coming faster and faster, and more and more accurately. Never perfect, mind you, but increasingly on the mark.

Even older than Taoism, the Chinese art of arranging one's personal environment, *Feng Shui* - which has become fashionable lately in this country when architectural or interior-design decisions are made about a home or workplace - would have me try to arrange my immediate physical environment to be more nurturing of my growing intuition.

Could intuition *be* my *Teh*? Is this what the universe is trying to give me, to tell me? Moving my insights that are initially unconscious up to the conscious realm would help me answer those questions.

As I said, as I have matured I have learned to take my intuitions more seriously. From simple "premonitions" that I should not drive my car on a certain day to a specified place - and not following this strange feeling has nearly gotten me killed a few times; to hunches about the guilt or innocence of people charged with murder - I knew instantly and felt certain, for instance, that Susan Smith had killed her two little children in North Carolina, even when the rest of the world believed her tearful story that a black man had kidnapped them from her car; to more complicated intuitions about the health or safety of my own children...

One example of this: I knew, while reading a book many miles away, the instant that my younger son was injured on a bicycle, and searched for him until I drove up to a small hospital in Madison, WI, that I did not even know existed. I just kept turning the steering wheel of my car left and right until there he was, in the hospital doorway with his mother and him gaping at me in wonder.

Recently, roaming the Internet has ironically given me more appreciation of similar inner struggles by other people. The Web itself is being used by some as a tool for self-direction, even if that means hiding behind the screen. These techies know that there is always some kind of screen anyway between the rational mind and everything else.

But how can "psychic" experience jive with science as well as logic? Easily, and even rats can do it. The bridge between subjective "ideas" or even "emotions" and the real world out there seems to have already been found: the electrical pulses of the brain, any brain. *Business Week*

(July 12, 1999, p. 139) reported research on thirsty rats that

> *just think about doing it [don't actually press a lever that dispenses water], and an electrode in their brain picks up the signal that used to go to their muscles - and activates the arm directly... the technology [might] enable people to control artificial limbs by brain impulses alone.*

We know from our own cell phones that the end points of two-way electromagnetic communication do not have to be physically connected to each other. We should now catch up with those lab rats and drop the telegraph model of communicating over distance.

Had I appreciated the fact, in years past, that both contemporary science and modern logic allow intuition a legitimate role in a rational, well-educated modern mind, I would have explored the power of my constant intuitions long ago. Only recently have I begun to apply intuition to my own career and to money questions. But perhaps that is because, in the household of my childhood, issues of economic security were crazymakers. The extreme thrift of those bad old days has been balanced off since then, in my personal psyche, by my extreme tendency to spend and to look the other way on money matters. Well, that has to change too, through logical if not intuitive means.

Even computers need to become intuitive or at least intuitionist. Example: ever since I "upgraded" my word processing program, it absolutely refuses to let me type the word *Teh* (though I've learned how to deal with it), always automatically changing my stupid error to *The*. But "The" and "Virtue" are not the same thing, not things at all!

But can my own family and I survive if I am actualizing intuition rather than earning more and more money through my analytic abilities? No one (not even the ancient Maya) would pay a living wage to someone like me to go around having intuitive experiences. But perhaps I should spend some of my time trying to predict the stock market! Maybe I always knew how to win the rat race after all. All my brain has to do is to think the predictions, then project the right impulses.

The Same Volcano

All this brings to mind that three of my great heroes spent much of their lives in the money business: Wallace Stevens, a poet quoted on "clouds" at the end of the last chapter, and much concerned with the order found in harmony, was a vice president at a life insurance company; Benjamin Lee Whorf - the part-time linguist who introduced me to the alternative philosophies inherent in traditional American Indian languages - also worked in an insurance company, which did not prevent him from making major contributions to Aztec, Mayan, and Hopi linguistics as well.

Franz Kafka studied law and then labored in the government workers' compensation office, which no doubt deeply inspired some of his greatest works, like *The Trial* and *The Castle*.

No, I am not going to start selling insurance, but I do need a better balance between my left brain's analytic work (highly valued by my yang-dominated capitalist culture) and my right brain's nonlinear ability. If intuitive insight is my Virtue it will grow out of the tensions between these "opposite" mental aptitudes or tendencies. As Stevens once remarked, "Description is revelation," so here goes...

Some years ago a couple of friends of mine temporarily solved the economic pressures by joining a Pennsylvania group that followed the teachings of Gurdjieff and his interpreter Ouspensky. I visited them in their forested, exceedingly modest retreat, but concluded they were missing out on one of Gurdjieff's excessive abilities - his instinct for raising money and keeping a grip on it! And for this he was roundly criticized in the years before and since his death in 1945. But as we look back at him from the new millennium, he was not asleep at the wheel. Robert Louis Stevenson reminds us that even "art is, first of all and last of all, a trade."

Perhaps left and right, analytic and intuitive are simplistic distinctions if conceptualized in the typical dualistic manner. These tendencies might someday be thought of as polarities, or even just part of a larger "modular" organization of the brain, as the recent Modular Theory maintains. More simply put is Arthur C. Clarke's view in his science-fiction story, "Dog Star": "The human mind has strange and labyrinthine ways of going about its business."

I also recall again that other theory, known as Complexity, by coincidence or by synchronicity studied around Santa Fe, a theory which should make me question whether I can even pretend to know what intuition is. (Residents like to call Santa Fe "the city different," which it certainly is, but I like to call it "the synchronous city.") Perhaps intuition is my personal midpoint between chaos and order; perhaps, indeed, it is my own Golden Mean as well as the balancing of my personal extremes. But I suppose that how I behave from now on is more significant than how I end up describing it.

If I become a self-employed fundraising consultant, I will have to be the only one responsible for my results or lack thereof. What I need to do is to create a kind of "rolling" consultancy, in which I always have two or more contractors, and whenever I lose or complete one assignment I find another to replace it and its income. That will demand great flexibility from me, and make me responsible for balancing or not balancing my life and especially my time.

I hope that my intuitive powers can also help me make the frequent and fast decisions that will be needed concerning which people and organizations I should work for. For a constantly permutating kaleidoscope of jobs means making good decisions about the character of my possible employers, evaluating the organization's mission, the time commitment I must make to each, the income I can earn in total, and other aspects of an employment Gestalt. The more I think about being a consultant, the more I realize that my success will hinge on how well my intuitive and logical abilities work together.

Some people prefer to emphasize "instinct" rather than intuition when they talk about the non-logical side of the human mind. In her book, *Pure Instinct* (Times Books, 1993), Kathy Kolbe begins by quoting another of my favorite American philosophers, William James, a proponent of respecting the role of the "other side" of our minds without losing balance with the more rational side. According to James, "The animal richest in reason might be also the animal richest in instinctive impulses."

For Kolbe, instincts are "innate, action-oriented, subconscious, protective, definitely not learned, and clearly a necessity." As she defines it, "The Creative Process... is the path that integrates otherwise separate elements of the mind's capacity: the abilities to act with motivation, determination, and reason" (p. 23).

This is a very important way to put the point. In no way am I advocating irrationalism to off-set Western analytic rationalism; rather, it is instinct and intuition, in mutual respect for and dependency with logic, that need to find a respected place in my mind. This is to balance, not neutralize, my reasoning capacity.

In the end, such counterbalancing of my mental faculties will result in a *stronger* reasoning capacity, for it focuses the latter on its proper subject matter, as Hume recommends we do. And this strengthening and focusing will only increase my ability to criticize and analyze and move past society's current models of how to succeed.

For our world today might very well be the last world, our final attempt at harmony in the midst of the irrational destruction of Earth's nature and humanity.

Seeds of Light

Previously in my Wayfaring journey as recorded in this book, I took inspiration from a Christian monk, Thomas Merton. In that part of the journey on the *Tao*, which we have seen has many other names both Eastern and Western, it became evident that Nietzsche was wrong when he said the last Christian died on the cross. Indeed, in the first book I ever read on the history of philosophy, *The Story of Philosophy*, Will Durant said the same thing about the Jewish philosopher, Spinoza.

Long before I ever thought about these things, or about what role intuition has or should have in my life, Spinoza was living his own balanced life, with the modes of his very modest Dutch existence (writing books and grinding lenses) in harmony with his intellectual intuition of the unity of God, or all of nature - from the perspective of eternity.

Of special significance to me is the way that Spinoza - contrary to the popular image of him, then and now - seems to have balanced a rigorous, nearly geometrical intellect with a Christ-like ability to empathize with ("imitate") the pains and pleasures of others. In a religious mind like his, the ego is not an obstacle but a gateway to freedom.

But I do not find inspiration in other, much more recent Christians who have somehow become the best-publicized religious force today - the right-wing fundamentalists. Reason requires a distinction between these theocrats and the more pious Christians known as evangelicals. In referring now to fundamentalism, I am thinking of such political forces as the Christian Coalition.

Their now-forgotten Contract with the American Family - which they called the Ten Suggestions - included allowing prayer in public places, even in government locations such as courthouses.

Aside from violating the Constitutional (and the

Founding Fathers') separation of church and state, and all that history has proven about theocracy, the right-wing fundamentalist political agenda still does not balance their extreme beliefs with any rational respect for the political or religious beliefs of others. Political extremism without an equal balance (that is, without harmony), is called fanaticism. It ought to be obvious by now that such one-sided extremism, as well as similar endeavors to fully control other living beings, violate Wayfaring.

But, unlike Nietzsche, I for one believe Christians do have a good point to make, and it's about redemption, or at least redeeming oneself. Christianity cuts you some slack when you need it. But it is in nature that we can also locate this redemptive quality. Maybe now *is* the right time to look again at nature's capacity, in partnership with humans, to do this.

I had a spooky experience about redemption once. In the first days of January 1985 I was driving in the middle of the night all alone through Utah, and at about two a.m. I was getting drowsy as I approached Green River. At least at that time, there were almost no gas stations or restaurants for long, long periods, but at night it is cooler there and I needed to make Time (of course).

Anyway, I turned on the radio and looked for a station that could keep me awake until I could find some food and coffee in the town ahead of me, and so I settled on one of those rural, right-wing preachers, yelling so loudly and offensively (to this one listener) that I snapped right to attention. "Redemption!! Redemption!!" he screamed, right before he asked for donations in a much quieter tone of voice.

Then, for about 30 seconds, I thought I had actually died and gone to hell. Now, in the distance, I saw a bright green neon sign, blinking on and off, on and off, but it did not get me sleepy again. That was because I could swear it was blinking "Redemption!!" in perfect harmony with the Christian preacher on the radio.

I thought to myself: Either that is true, and God is trying to give me a hint, or I fell asleep at the wheel, crashed my car, and went straight to hell, where my lack of belief in this preacher's brimstone would force me to view that brightly lit, greenish-yellow warning sign over and over, forever and ever.

But in just a few more seconds, I found myself still alive and driving my car into the outskirts of Green River, where on the side of one of the first buildings I approached there was a huge, broken neon sign, and only the one word, "Redemption", was lit - the other words must have burnt out long ago. Those other words, etched from cold glass, were "S & H Green Stamp... Center."

When I had recovered, I started thinking of my favorite old Western movies, which all seem to have redemption as their theme. The Western part of the West still has much to teach me.

But I don't want to get too irrational here. Excesses of emotion and experience must balance off each other. Many a philosophy of life has been commandeered and misappropriated by irrationalism. For instance, the proto-Nazis in Germany (pseudo-intellectuals who had a big influence on Hitler) right before World War I believed that:

Imagination, feeling, and will attributed to Natural Man, were placed above reason, which was held responsible for the psychic disorders of civilized man. The irrational was recognized as a source of illumination.
(D. Sklar, *The Nazis and the Occult*, Dorset Press, 1989, p. 14)

Asian philosophies, occult or not, can also be utilized by irrationalists. Even Taoism can be used this way, as some of the characters do in Philip K. Dick's classic science fiction novel, *The Man in the High Castle* (1962). But, in Chapter 7, this horror story of life on Earth after the Nazis and the Japanese win World War II also gives us a glimpse of the original face of Taoism:

What would it be like... to really know the Tao? The Tao is that which first lets the light, then the dark. *Occasions the interplay of the two primal forces so that there is always renewal. It is that which keeps it all from wearing down.* The universe will never be extinguished because just when the darkness seems to have smothered all, to be truly transcendent, the new seeds of light are reborn in the very depths. That is the Way. *When the seed falls, it falls into the earth, into the soil. And beneath, out of sight, it comes to life.*

As I have been stressing, the very heart of counterbalancing is the *equal* tension between our extremes - in my own case, between logic and intuition or instinct. *It is this balancing or harmonizing of the extremes of our energies that results in illumination... in light.* And it is exactly this equal balancing that is so difficult to achieve: First, because we have to fight against the long Aristotelian tradition that the moderate, in-between compromise is human rationality itself, and also against the corollary - that the extremes (in my case) of intuitions or instincts are the essence of irrationality.

Second, balancing is tough because we need to learn and relearn what our own extreme states, feelings, emotions, intuitions and instincts really are; third, because it takes time to set ourselves right, to know when our instincts are out of balance with each other; and lastly, as Spinoza emphasized via his geometrical presentations, because all of these realizations *about* the intuitive side require reasoning, and so an even higher balance between instinct and reason is possible.

Go back, take away the emotions, learn from the experiences, and pure reason returns. With perfect reason comes intuition. With perfect intuition comes a complete understanding...
(Leandis, *in Shadowcatchers*, by Steve Wall, Harper Collins: 1994, pp. 33-34)

I also now recall the English writer De Quincey's defense, in his *Confessions of an English Opium-Eater* (1821), of referring to himself as a "philosopher": an analytic thinker who possesses "the *moral* faculties, as shall give him an inner eye and power of intuition for the vision and the mysteries of our human nature..."

Clearly, I personally will have to rely on intuition and instinct, in balance with logic, to know what combination of job assignments will be most conducive to my greater self-balancing.

The film *Instinct* puts a lot of these themes together as only a film can. The extremist who finds the right job - living with mountain gorillas in the jungle mists of Africa - fights off the entire Western assumption that we must control other beings or *be* controlled by them: the either/or. Through the growing empathy of a psychiatrist, the instincts of each man open up to the other.

But that is just one way the extremes of feeling and thinking can manifest themselves in people.

The extremes that I might find in one job can be balanced by "opposites" found in another job.

The effects of one very macho boss might be balanced by the contributions of a laid-back boss in a different, concurrent fundraising assignment. Because there is not enough time to investigate and confirm the presence of such attributes in potential bosses, intuition and instinct are essential here.

But so is the logic of reason. As I will also need balance among the fields in which I work, my logical abilities are required to figure out, for example, that an educational institution, an international relations group, and an environmental organization would constitute a good balance (all other things being equal, knowledge of which also requires reasoning) in my fundraising work.

These fields are completely separate from each other (at least for fundraising purposes) and, as such, will present "opposite" types of extreme emotions and behaviors as well as preclude any conflicts of interest when I approach major funding sources.

Edgar Allan Poe helps me out again, specifically his first words in *The Murders in the Rue Morgue*:

> *The mental features discoursed of as the analytical are, in themselves, but little susceptible of analysis. We appreciate them only in their effects. We know of them, among other things, that they are always to their possessor, when inordinately possessed, a source of the liveliest enjoyment. As the strong man exults in his physical ability, delighting in such exercises as call his muscles into action, so glories the analyst in that moral activity which disentangles. He derives pleasure from even the most trivial occupations bringing his talent into play. He is fond of enigmas, of conundrums, of hieroglyphics; exhibiting in his solutions of each a degree of acumen which appears to the ordinary apprehension preternatural. His results, brought about by the very soul and essence of method, have, in truth, the whole air of intuition.*
>
> *...It will be found, in fact, that the ingenious are always fanciful, and the truly imaginative never otherwise than analytic.*

It strikes me that Poe may view the analytic and the intuitive as a continuum, in no way antagonistic to each other. In any case, once I get my own "mental features" into better balance, I can do a better job of helping the rest of the world, including the living things in and on my lawn.

This paradigm of the continuum of life logically implies extremes at either end, or no ends at all! The great Platonists, from Plato himself down to Kurt Gödel, were both analytic logicians and highly intuitive people - there is no disagreement on that point.

I too just had two astonishing experiences in the

unexplored region between (or above) analysis and intuition or instinct. Perhaps these are more examples of what Jung called "synchronicity." Both of these insights came from looking up non-Western words in Western reference works.

In checking the entry on "Maya" in *The Columbia Encyclopedia* (Fifth Edition, 1993), I inadvertently hit upon the Indian word "maya" (with a small "m") on the same page (1,728): in Hinduism, term used in the Veda to mean magic or supernatural power. In Mahayana Buddhism it acquires the meaning of illusion or unreality. The term is pivotal in the Vedanta system of Shankara, where it signifies the world as a cosmic illusion and also the power that creates the world.

Power as force or power as *Teh*?

Then there is the other coincidence I just had. After all the years I have been thinking about the concept of "yin," and after all my tribulations over the lawn, here's what I read, for the very first time, in the *Shambhala Dictionary of Taoism* (Shambhala: 1996, p. 217):

Originally the word yin *designated the northern slope of a mountain, i.e., the side facing away from the sun - and was further associated with... a cloud-covered sky.*

My yin-oriented, erosion-prone backyard happens to be a steep northern slope. Strange coincidence? That word is just the analytic side of intuition's synchronicity. Moreover, as a plain matter of fact, I was unaware of the etiology of "yin" whenever I referred previously to the lawn or the mountains or the clouds.

Selective ignorance has always been a convenient Taoist tool!

According to the Taoist known as Zhao, an Immortal Sister of the Song dynasty in China nearly a thousand years ago, people I call Wayfarers live in all parts of the Earth. Moreover,

Some of them take care of rivers and lakes, some of them manage the hidden government, some are in charge of mountains. They work to benefit ten thousand generations, to rid the earth of what is harmful...
(IS, p. 5)

Another weird synchronicity or coincidence taught me how good people can be in charge of mountains, in a way. In 1986, I was visiting my son who was staying with his uncle in Marin County, California. This uncle was a plumbing contractor (a contractor, he claimed, not a mere plumber), and as I have been forced to mention, I had done some plumbing, in fact with him and his father (by then deceased) many years earlier. So when an emergency call came in to fix a broken pipe, I accompanied him and we took off. The residence was a lovely home almost at the top of Mt. Tamalpais, called Mt. Tam by the locals.

While working there I noticed an old photo on an even older desk in a side room, and somehow it seemed familiar. I went up to it - it was a fading picture of Alan Watts (quoted above on Chinese yin/yang), along with a few of his friends. I thought to myself: Surely this coincidence is not possible!

For Alan Watts has always been a real inspiration to me, beginning at the age of 15 when I read *The Way of Zen*. The first Zen quotes, my first *koans*, came to me from this wonderful book.

Anyway, it turned out that this was the very house in which Watts had done a lot of his best writing over the years, before he passed away in 1973. The current resident confirmed all this, told me about Watts' pals, and took me to Watts' meditation rock overlooking the valley.

Later I found a cover photo on one of my Watts books at home, and there he was, perched on that stone on that mountain, looking peaceful, or least the valley did.

What made me go up there? It was the only time I ever helped out my son's uncle on a plumbing job. And, as with my visit, so to speak, to the Zen monastery in New

Mexico, fixing water pipes was not, and still is not, my idea of how to relax out West.

There is a story in the *Washington Post* of June 2, 1999 (p. C9) about John Cowden and his family, who, though they had failed at raising cattle, sheep, and Christmas trees (but apparently not at plumbing) on their 3,200 acres in western Virginia, knew how to take care of natural things:

> *In 1984, while restoring the 1850s gristmill on the property and figuring out what to do next, John had a sort of revelation.*
> *"Rather than force the land to do something it's not suited for, I decided to look at the land and ask what it was best suited for," he says.*
> *The answer was a hybrid: a lodge..., a country inn....[a]nd some cows, because the land liked to grow grass and he'd be damned if he was going to mow it every week.*

My own transition to a new work lifestyle, a new branch - like my efforts to transform the lawn itself - will take time (the intangible) and money (the tangible). In practicing occasional *wu wei* toward my culture's rigid economic demands, I will face great financial uncertainty. But it will be worth it if I can unify my spatial and temporal dimensions or at least harmonize them. I have to begin today to start thinking about money and work in a different light, according to a model that is different from others', more like saving water and planting rocks in Las Vegas.

But sometimes, being different is being traditional, going way back in spacetime, perhaps to an ancient female tribal leader who is one of Taoism's oldest legends. In some remote period, she "patched the sky with five-colored stones" in order to try to bring back the "harmony with nature [that] had been lost" (*IS*, p. 2). Her work is not done.

But she would be proud of the female authors whose nature writings are compiled in books like *Sisters of the Earth* (ed. by Lorraine Anderson, Vintage: 1991). That volume quotes the Creek Indian poet Joy Harjo as she speaks about being a woman:

she must know
the voices of mountains
she must recognize
the foreverness of blue sky ...
i am a continuance
of blue sky ...
                    (p. 3)

The Resurrection of Space and Time

Unmanifest Destiny

What I need soon are some really good coincidences, which I now believe might be helped along by a new language of reality, my here-and-now, as their "process" language does for Hopis... at least our word "process" seems to be as close as we are going to get to the Hopi Way as described by B. L. Whorf. George Johnson says that the implications of this Hopi world view "seem almost Einsteinian" (p. 205). For example, he points out that

Whorf studied the language of the Tewa's distant cousins, the Hopi, concluding that they have no words for time...

...Whorf concluded that in place of time and space or past and future, the Hopi divided everything into what he called the Manifest and the Manifesting (or, alternately, the Unmanifest).

(*Fire in the Mind*, pp. 205, 204)

I do have to appreciate how my language (that most powerful of all screens) constrains my choices. Like Hopi and Tewa, as different from each other in origins and structure as both are from English, the Mayan language also suggests different options for me:

The principal language of our reality here in the West is economics. Important issues in our lives, such as progress and social justice, war and peace, and the hope for prosperity and security, are expressed in material metaphors. Struggles, both moral and military, between

the haves and have-nots of our world pervade our public media and our thoughts of the future. The Maya codified their shared model of reality through religion and ritual rather than economics. The language of Maya religion explained the place of human beings in nature, the workings of the sacred world, and the mysteries of life and death, just as our religion still does for us in special circumstances like marriages and funerals. But their religious system also encompassed practical matters of political and economic power, such as how the ordered world of the community worked.

(Schele and Freidel, *A Forest of Kings: The Untold Story of the Ancient Maya*, Quill William Morrow: 1990, p. 65.)

That the Maya alternative metaphor of language and therefore of existence is so little known and appreciated nowadays is shown in an article in *The Washington Post* on May 12, 1999, an account of what life must have been like for people living at the turn of another millennium, in 999 A.D. Various great cultures are discussed - in Europe, Asia Minor, the Middle East, even a brief nod toward China and India - but not a single word about the cultures here in the Americas, which were in some ways (and Ways) far ahead of the more familiar pillars of the West. These reporters, who deal in the coin of language, need to just keep traveling even farther west! The Western and Eastern extremes are crucial to understanding our potential future as well as our true past.

What can be proved within and through language is less than the capacity of human thought. This, in turn, is less (weaker) than what is possible in the world.

(*Gödel*, Casti and DePauli, p. 73)

Fun Raising

One last story, my longest, will give an example of how a Western approach can also offer Zen-like clarity and humor about language and how it can first limit, then open up our choices.

Although it's true I have never sold insurance, even if some of our finest writers have, I did sell encyclopedias for a few months, virtually door-to-door. When I quit academia, and before I got my first job in fundraising, I thought of encyclopedias - the repository of Western wisdom at least since the Enlightenment (the European kind), and the symbol in some ways of my former university life - and earning money by selling them to the knowledge-starved public.

It was a tough way to earn a few dollars, though I was in good company, such as the great country singer/song writer Willie Nelson, who also sold encyclopedias elsewhere. But years later, I was presented with a different view of the many roles that selling encyclopedias can play.

I had become, at that later time, head of development for an environmental organization focusing on getting businesses to be energy efficient. I had the bright idea, I thought, of finding one giant company, like the Walt Disney Company, that would announce it would become energy efficient, and eventually adopt efficient light bulbs and heating systems and other ways to protect against climate change and the pollution of nature, including people.

Through old friends working at Disney, I left a message for Frank Wells, then the president of the company, who was to die tragically a few years later in a helicopter accident while "extreme skiing." Believe it or not, he returned my call from his car phone. I told him what I had in mind, he expressed strong interest (he himself was known to be an environmentalist) and invited me and the top officers of my nonprofit organization to fly out that very week and have breakfast with him and his environmental staff at his home.

That Friday morning in Beverly Hills, the boss of my organization got a bit flustered, for whatever reason, while introducing our staff, and when he got to me he completely forgot my title and duties but remembered, so help me, what I used to do long before.

He announced to Mr. Wells and the top environmental staff of the Walt Disney Company: "This is Rich Spiegel... who... used to... sell a lot of encyclopedias."

After the laughter died down, Frank Wells said: "Then Rich is the most qualified person to represent your organization today." This time there was dead silence, except for my sudden outburst of laughter, then Wells slowly cracked a smile, and then everyone was in stitches.

No, I did not get any money from Disney, but ever since that day - when Wells served as the guide through our spacetime - I have had a different view of getting, gaining and selling wisdom.

Heart of Sky

A more poetical approach to "opening up" time and space is suggested by Dennis Tedlock in the preface to his edition of the *Popol Vuh* (Touchstone: 1986, p. 21), the "bible" of the Maya of the late classic period. The editor's Quiche mentor wanted to add, in part, the following lines to the public prayer of the "daykeepers:"

> ...*and may the sifting of ancient times*
> *be complete in my heart, in my head;*
> *and make my guilt vanish,*
> *my grandmothers, grandfathers,*
> *and however many souls of the dead there may be,*
> *you who speak with the [gods] Heart of Sky and Earth,*
> *may all of you together give strength*
> *to the reading I have undertaken.*

And to this writing that I have undertaken, and to the Way that has overtaken me.

We can talk about nature, our ultimate home, as spiritual or as material or both. The grass below my feet is greening, the sky above me blues, the blue around me is clouding up, the wind vanishes clouds like guilt. None of these events is purely in space or just in time. "They" exist only in their consequences. That's why this world, our last world, can become a lasting world.

But nature is what it is, nature naturing and nature nurturing. Nature no more means "good" than "man-made" means bad. Edgar Allan Poe, like Baudelaire and van Gogh after him, relied on the "natural" green liqueur absinthe to get by, even though we now know that it contains a neurotoxin (also in wormwood oil) that can create hallucinations and even convulsions.

Such great artists, like my lawn, have to take the risks inherent in growing wild yet not totally so. I too have to know how extreme, how far out, I can really go, physically, emotionally and financially, and still retain the overall harmony, the self-directedness, that allows the flowering of *Teh*. While I can and will help the lawn, as a natural whole, find and follow its balance of extremes, nature can in turn continue to help me find my own Way.

One thing that will really help me do that is not to worry so much about making mistakes, whatever they are! The ingrained dualism of right vs. wrong in our action and even in our thinking can prevent me from learning in yin ways, described by Ray Grigg in these words:

> ...*the Tao is essentially discovered by learning what not to be and do. Mistakes, therefore, become a valuable source of information - perhaps the only source.*
> (*The Tao of Zen*, Alva Press: 1994, p. 233)

So it follows that I should make as many mistakes as I can! Another approach I can follow is Alexander Pope's, offered in *An Essay on Man*:

All nature is but art, unknown to thee;
All chance, direction, which thou canst not see;
All discord, harmony, not understood....

Well, now, as I look at my backyard, I see for the first time that it does have a direction, a trajectory so to speak, which has become clear to me only after years of observation: believe it or not, the whole high hill in back is slowly, patiently, and inexorably shifting forward! Lately I have noticed that the ground in back is moving toward, or perhaps eventually even over, the front. What a surprise that would be.

Soil is accumulating on the steps going from the deck to the back yard, creeping toward us inch by inch. The erosion, which I assumed was a negative, a lack of something material, is turning out to be a force in itself or at least to have forceful consequences. The extremes are becoming each other. And they do not come to be without their partner, their polarity. That is the only completeness it, or we, can know.

A golden apple tree that my wife and I recently planted in back is growing happily, but leaning far backward, so the earth shift is clearly deep and not just with the looser soil on top. Lately when I have been cooking breakfast in the early morning, I see that the water in the pot is tilting toward the side of the stove facing the front yard. Where will it all stop? Or should I say, When?

Even my black locust, pivot of the landscape, seems closer to me now than when I began these reflections. This very evening I cut down some of its dead branches, and of course I was very careful not to harm the tree or the shrubs or even the vines surrounding it, but less careful with myself - a thorn on the locust cut my finger. Something happens every time. The other side of power, I guess.

Meanwhile, a resident cardinal is taking advantage of a gust of wind and landing on one of the large dead branches I was not able to reach, to check on my work, it seems. I'm glad it's not an expert bower bird, because my branch-trimming of the locust was not exactly elegant.

I did a little better with the chalk maple and the white pine standing between the house and the new apple tree, on the side opposite Jack's guard station. It looks like the maple is growing so fast and wide it is starting to crowd the more modest pine. One side of the conifer is just starting to intertwine with the maple branches, some of which are almost touching the sloping ground. So I trimmed some of those and removed a bunch of broken twigs from the pine. Because the maple is a little lower down the hill, it normally receives more water than the higher-up pine. But the pine holds the water for a longer period, and is happier during a drought.

Over the years, the rose bushes have trimmed themselves to the remaining six that are flourishing next to a new jungle of delicious raspberries. But with my guidance, the delicate roses and the aggressive raspberries have decided to grow in different directions: live and let live. None of these plants seem very concerned about which direction they are moving in space or time, or in both or neither.

I think of Arthur Conan Doyle's story, "The Naval Treaty," in which Sherlock Holmes smells a rose and observes, "What a lovely thing a rose is!" After a comment on deduction, he says, "Our highest assurance of the goodness of Providence seems to me to rest in the flowers." Even the "world's greatest detective" and its most rigorous practical logician stops to smell the roses.

If the roses in front of me could look over their shoulders (or hips), up toward the growing saplings along the cliff edge, they would see some of the weird-looking caterpillar tents again. Those gray tents also seem closer than ever too, only they are not the gypsy-moth nurseries I thought they were. I just found out that they are tent caterpillars, completely harmless to my black locust though a mild threat to this year's roses. Wiping out that one bunch of infant tent moths some years ago turned out to be wrong, dead wrong, a case of mistaken identity, and an argument against the death penalty. The moral logic is the same, whoever or whatever may be the victim... or the killer.

Remember the Caterpillar's advice to Alice in *Alice's Adventures in Wonderland*? First he or it tells Alice (and me) to "Keep your temper." Then, as with the nursery rhyme that Alice tries to recite correctly, the Caterpillar points out that "It is wrong from beginning to end." That is about as morally categorical as one can get about my destruction of the tent caterpillars.

And the Caterpillar, speaking for all other caterpillars as well, poses the most puzzling question I have yet had to face these past years: "So you think you're changed, do you?"

Well, over the years the lawn has changed me in one obvious respect: some months ago, while trimming the raspberry bushes along the other side of Jack's area - just trying to create a straighter, more Euclidean line of sight from the roadway - I got poison ivy on my hands, then on my legs, and so on. The worst case I've had since I was a kid. The poison ivy came along with the remarkable amount of shrubbery, grass, flowers and young trees now filling the entire space below my black locust and all around it.

Speaking of kids, when it has snowed each winter, all at once the neighborhood gets friendly, and little children as well as very big teenagers swarm over the side of the white front yard with their sharp sleds and slippery tire tubes. Despite the permanent damage they do to the lawn (but apparently not to the ant hills), these contraptions and their screaming pilots seem to have no effect whatsoever on the next season's poison ivy crop.

But it's not worth earning the enmity of the whole neighborhood just to keep these kids from zooming down the hill over the glistening snow pack. I will keep my temper, because no one else deserves it.

Jack too keeps his temper around the kids of winter,

and off-sets the damage they do to the lawn by generously contributing a daily dose of fertilizer. That has helped that part of the lawn grow bright green, almost lime-green, though a bit spotty, as late winter is followed by early spring, then late spring, early summer, and sometimes the drought of late summer. The eight seasons of the ancient Chinese calendar make me think differently about how this planet, especially my lawn, changes each year.

Also on Jack's side of the lawn is a stack of old firewood, over which a pumpkin-like vine is growing by leaps and bounds, sometimes six inches a day, and is now climbing up the drainpipe of the house. All along it shoot out thin little tendrils searching for something to hold on to. Last week some tendrils at the head of the vine were just inches from the pine tree on that side of the house. How did they know that the pine branch in front of them was the closest of all the surrounding twigs and branches?

But by yesterday the lead tendrils were no longer pursuing that particular part of my old pine neighbor - maybe due to the increasing weight of the thickening vines and ever-widening leaves these searchers now have a tight grip around a lower branch. They might be tapping the bluish-green needles for water - tendril-pilgrims whose duty is to scout ahead while not risking the main body of the vine. Another set of tendrils has grasped onto some loose, unattached pine needles like a baseball glove stretching for a long ball. It looks like a great catch in mid-air.

This morning, a little cooler, with the breeze up and running, one enormous mustard-colored flower is blaring silently from that vine like a trumpet at dawn. It's beautiful to behold but will not hold up when it changes into a gourd, or calabash, in fall. Maybe I should have practiced a bit more *wu wei* toward my newest neighbor, who will be bearing loads much heavier than mine.

Seeing the residents of the plant and animal kingdom as our neighbors is beautifully articulated in Sarah Orne

Jewett's *The Country of the Pointed Firs*, the 1896 swan song of the Victorian relationship with nature. Or the heron song, as in another of her stories, "A White Heron."

The grass between and among all the growing plants in the back yard is now so thick that the water dropped by heavy rains on the very highest part of the hill, well back from and beyond my property line, likes to cascade down the slope and right over the grass and rest against the back of our house. Water is not just a metaphor anymore.

Grasping the Wind

Chuang Tzu had his butterfly-dream metaphor. The Caterpillar of Alice's Wonderland, you'll recall, also transforms into a butterfly, and butterflies, especially Monarchs, are considered to be "canaries in the mine" of the real world, signaling environmental dangers around us long before humans notice them. Monarch populations in their winter grounds west of Mexico City, to which they fly 1,000 miles or more according to their internal magnetic compass, are way down recently - one more alarm from nature.

But butterflies have much to teach us on the everyday level too. As I was hiking the other day, a golden flash of light caught my eye, contrasted against the dark macadam road surface. Thinking the brightness was just a dead leaf in the wind, I came up to the spot, and there in the street were two butterflies. One, a female, did not move and may have hit the windshield of a car tearing down this country road. On top was a larger male, very much alive, its wings fluttering desperately, its thin legs clutching the female. For all the world it looked like a husband trying to wake up his mate or to lift her off the road to a safer position.

Wu wei-like, I did not interfere, as any attempt on my part to help would mean certain damage to the gossamer of the male's wings, at the very least. But the most amazing thing is that as I peered closely at the life-and-death struggle, the male would just flutter some more... he was not going to abandon her, even if a terrifying thing 10,000 times his height loomed over them. Later when I circled around and came by again, the male had succeeded in reaching the grassy shoulder along with his final burden, but still he would not rest.

In the Bible (12:7-8), our old mentor Job insists on answers to some of these difficult and violent issues that all living things face, including hazards both to and from the environment, then and now, and the answers come to him "out of the whirlwind:"

Ask the beasts, and they will teach you;
the birds of the sky, they will tell you;
or speak to the earth, it will teach you;
the fish of the sea, they will inform you.

Now I notice two fat rabbits, a couple, nibbling away at something on the front lawn (not the ants, I'll bet), and clearly happy with things as they are here. This must be an upscale neighborhood for rabbits, even better than living under a golf course. So far they have "made it." And so has the lawn itself.

But it looks like the rabbits might be attracting company - a boisterous red-tailed hawk who hangs out on a dead branch near the top of the highest tree in back. With all the housing and commercial development around here, and its abundant road-kill, it's the turkey buzzards and the huge shiny crows that are enjoying the moveable feast, not the hawks, who have all but disappeared from the local scene. Until this one started coming occasionally to my backyard for breakfast.

Standing guard over all these changes, almost from the exact day I started writing down these reflections, is another beast who has taught me much. Jack, my gentle Rottweiler who now weighs almost 150 pounds. Jack would love to chase the rabbits, but he actually prefers to eat fruits and vegetables (I wonder if he likes pumpkins?), and will not chew on a bone or uncooked meat at all. And he prefers being inside, where he can catch flies from a dead sleep, leaping high into the air, snapping his jaws, and gingerly swallowing the flying snack. And anyway, inside the house he can at least try to hide from the thunder and lightning and loud wind that so terrify him during storms.

> *There abides the bitter wind.*
> *Not slowly did we go...*
> *I grasped the wind....*
> (From a Papago Indian song)

Jack complements my experience by sensing realities that I cannot. All I have to do is watch him sniffing the wind and listening to a world beyond my own. In turn, I share with him a moral reality which I definitely sense but which is only rudimentary in him, for now.

But we are about equal in empathic ability, a conclusion I base on the way he tries to run to the rescue of every crying child within a six-block radius of the backyard (something I do not do).

We are now also almost exactly equal in age. We both have occasional twinges of pain in our left legs, he in his paw, me in my big toe and knee. For each of us, dog and man, any excess weight is settling in around the middle of our torsos. But unlike me, Jack sleeps a great deal, probably preparing for that world-class hunt he seems to dream about so often, yipping and pedaling his legs in pursuit of whatever creature he will never catch up with.

Outside, meanwhile, the ants whose ancestors years ago made my front lawn their dirt-homes - which at first I was unable, then unwilling to eradicate - are back in force. The intervening generations no doubt moved into better ant-neighborhoods, but the young ones have returned to the old homestead. My wife and I planted a peach tree out front, and some irises and azaleas, surrounded by multi-colored rocks. The pretty orange hues of the ant hills make a nice contrast.

By recognizing the *Teh* of all the beasts and other residents, old and new, in and on and over and under my lawn, front and back, and by speaking to the earth forces, I see that there is much more going on in and around me than I ever realized, just as Dorothy sees in *The Wizard of Oz*, after she too is buffeted by the whirlwind.

A whirlwind happens to have a spiral pattern of energy and also a forward motion. The Argentine poet Jorge Luis Borges likes to appeal to time as spiral as well as to the whirlwind theme. And D. H. Lawrence has this to say:

Not I, not I, but the wind that blows through me!
A fine wind is blowing the new direction of Time.
If only I let it bear me, carry me, if only it carry me!
            (from *Song of a Man Who Has Come Through*)

I think differently now about John Lennon's words: "you can learn how to be you in time."

Can these winds carry me forward now, as in this conclusion of the creation story told by the Mbaya people of Paraguay?

As he grew, the true Namandu Father, the First Being, created his future paradise. He created the earth. But at first he lived in the primal winds. The primal wind in which our Father lived returns with the yearly return of the primal time-space, with the yearly recurrence of the time-space that was. As soon as the season that was has ended, the trumpet-vine tree bears flowers. The winds move on to the following time-space. New winds and a new space in time come into being. Comes the resurrection of space and time.
(From *The Red Swan*, edited by John Bierhorst; Indian
                                        Head: 1992, p. 38)

The first world and the last world are the same.